D0712800

The Art of War

Translations from the Asian Classics

TRANSLATED BY VICTOR H. MAIR

The Art of War

Sun Zi's MILITARY METHODS

COLUMBIA UNIVERSITY PRESS NEW YORK

Columbia University Press
Publishers Since 1893
New York   Chichester, West Sussex

Copyright © 2007 Columbia University Press

Library of Congress Cataloging-in-Publication Data

Sunzi, 6th cent. B.C.
[Sunzi bing fa. English]
The art of war / Sun Zi's military methods ; translated by Victor H. Mair.
p. cm. — (Translations from the Asian Classics)
Includes bibliographical references and index.
ISBN 978-0-231-13382-1 (cloth) : alk. paper) — ISBN 978-0-231-50853-7 (e-book)
1. War—Early works to 1800. 2. Military art and science—Early works to 1800. I. Title.
U101.S9513 2007
355.02—dc22
2007017771
♾

Columbia University Press books are printed on permanent and
durable acid-free paper.
This book is printed on paper with recycled content.
Printed in the United States of America

c 10 9 8 7 6 5 4 3 2 1

Frontispiece

A type of bronze basin called a *jian*, which has a wide mouth, rounded sides, a flat
bottom, and four animal-head handles with movable rings. The outer surface
of the basin is covered with copper-inlaid battle scenes. This finely made *jian*
dates to the period from the late seventh through the early fifth centuries B.C.,
and was excavated from Tomb M1 at Shanbiao Zhen, Ji County, Henan Province. The *jian* here is one of a nearly identical pair, famous for their depiction
of battle in the period just before the compilation of the *Sun Zi bingfa*. They
provide important data for the study of the history of ancient weapons and early
warfare. We may note in particular that the soldiers in these scenes are armed
with bows instead of the crossbows, which had become popular by the time of
the *Sun Zi bingfa*. The illustrations in the text are based on rubbings taken from
this *jian*. It is housed in the Museum of the Institute of History and Philology
of Academia Sinica, Taipei, Taiwan, and published here with the permission of
the Institute. This impressive basin is also the source of the chapter designs.

Art on the title and dedication pages is by Daniel Heitkamp

For Li-ching
A Brave Fighter

CONTENTS

A good warrior is not bellicose,
A good fighter does not anger.
—*Tao te Ching/Dao de jing,* 68

The Way of heaven
    does not war
        yet is good at conquering.
—*Tao te Ching/Dao de jing,* 73

Now,
    Weapons are instruments of evil omen;
    Creation abhors them.
Therefore,
    One who aspires to the Way
        does not abide in them.

    The superior man
        at home honors the left,
        on the battlefield honors the right.

Therefore,
    Weapons are not instruments of the superior man;
    Weapons are instruments of evil omen,
        to be used only when there is no other choice.

    He places placidity above all
        And refuses to prettify weapons;
    If one prettifies weapons,
        This is to delight in the killing of others.

Now,
> One who delights in the killing of others
> Cannot exercise his will over all under heaven.

For this reason,
> On occasions for celebration,
>> the left is given priority;
> On occasions for mourning,
>> the right is given priority.

Therefore,
> A deputy general stands on the left,
> The general-in-chief stands on the right.
In other words,
> They stand in accordance with mourning ritual.

> The killing of masses of human beings,
>> we bewail with sorrow and grief;
> Victory in battle,
>> we commemorate with mourning ritual.
>> —*Tao te Ching*/*Dao de jing*, 31

Sun Wu . . . was a wise general of a former age. He is remote and recondite, and it is difficult to know anything about him.
> —Falsely attributed to Liu Xiang (79–78 B.C.),
> *Xin xu* (Newly compiled stories) and quoted in *Taiping yulan*
> (Imperial survey of the Great Peace [reign period];
> completed 984 A.D.), s. 276.

Arthur Waldron

Sun Zi was an extraordinary thinker, still very influential. As a strategist he shares supremacy with just one other writer: Carl von Clausewitz (1780–1831), author of *On War* (1832). Like Clausewitz, Sun Zi is unfortunately most familiar at second hand, through a handful of quotations that lack context, for like Clausewitz, he, too, is rarely read in his entirety, with real care. One reason for this is the great difficulty of translating either of these works into lucid English in a way that is true to the texts. *Vom Kriege* is difficult enough. Not until 1976 did a first-rate translation appear, by Michael Howard and Peter Paret.[1]

The problems faced by the translator of Sun Zi—textually, philologically, and in every other respect (save length)—are, however, orders of magnitude greater. Many fine scholars have attempted the task, and several excellent versions are already published. This one, however, stands out above the others. I am deeply honored to be invited to offer a foreword to this English version of Sun Zi, by my colleague Victor Mair, which I am confident will become the standard, both because of the deep understanding of the text that it manifests and because of its great clarity and readability.

To begin at the beginning: The title of Sun Zi's text, *bingfa* 兵法, is usually put into English as "the art of war," which suggests a closeness of theme to Clausewtiz's *Vom Kriege*, which unquestionably means "on war." But *bing* in Chinese usually means soldier, and Sun Zi, as Mair makes clear in his notes and as is evident from the text, is almost entirely concerned with military methods that can lead to victory, rather than with war as a general phenomenon. In his first chapter Sun Zi says a certain amount about the importance of war to the state and the perils of waging it unsuccessfully. But he is not concerned, as Clausewitz is, to isolate the philosophical essence of war, in the manner that German philosophers among his contemporaries did, in their studies of history, aesthetics, morals, or similar topics.

Clausewitz has a good deal to say about the operational and tactical issues involved in winning a war, and comparing Sun Zi to him at these points is very useful. But no explicit counterpart exists in Sun Zi to the carefully articulated philosophical framework about the fundamental nature of war that Clausewitz develops. One can, however, deduce Sun Zi's views on some of these issues.

Consider the question of the nature of war itself. Clausewitz had "first encountered war in 1793 as a twelve-year-old lance corporal" fighting the French, a task to which he was devoted until the final defeat of Napoleon at Waterloo thirty-two years later.[2] The Napoleonic Wars, though punctuated by truces and the forming and re-forming of coalitions, were essentially continuous and protracted over decades. They provided vivid lessons in the way that no single battle, no matter how decisive it might seem—either Austerlitz or Trafalgar, both in 1805, for example—seemed ever to be genuinely conclusive. They showed how the use of force elicited counterforce, and how the scale of that force might be driven up by this reciprocal action, in what today is called "escalation." The central importance of politics and the interaction between politics and the use of force was also clear in the Napoleonic Wars, particularly with respect to truces, the formation and maintenance of coalitions, and, in the final years, the issue of war aims with respect to Napoleon—could he be allowed to stay on as emperor in France, or was "unconditional surrender" (a term not yet in use) the goal?

From his experience of prolonged, escalating, and politically determined war, Clausewitz drew some of his most famous conclusions. What is war, in essence? His reply: "War is an act of force, and there is no logical limit to the application of that force. Each side, therefore, compels its opponent to follow suit; a reciprocal action is started which must lead, in theory, to extremes."[3] "War does not consist of a single short blow";[4] "In war the result is never final";[5] and, most famously, though the phrase can only be understood properly within the context that Clausewitz provides, "War is not merely an act of policy but a true political instrument, a continuation of political intercourse, carried on with other means. *What remains peculiar to war is simply the peculiar nature of its means.*"[6]

Clausewitz's fundamental concern is that unless they are firmly controlled by a political authority outside the military and having a fixed end in mind, the means by which war is waged—the application and counterapplication of force—will simply by their own interaction drive or escalate the conflict to a level of intensiveness and destruction that was not desired by either combatant and is not in either of their interests.

In Clausewitz's time, the ability to wage long, difficult, and ultimately decisive campaigns was all important. Troops and money could be found by the nation-states of late-eighteenth- and early-nineteenth-century Europe. By contrast, in the China of Sun Zi's time, nothing like the decades of conflict with Napoleon was possible. Simply to raise a single army taxed any state to the limit. If it was to have any political usefulness, violence therefore had to be concentrated in a handful of encounters, with rapid decision the goal.

This fact goes some way toward explaining the differences between the ways the two authors look at war in general. For Clausewitz it is above all a test of force. For Sun Zi it is more a psychological contest, with force having a far more limited role. For Clausewitz, war and fighting are, by their very nature, protracted. Sun Zi's ideal is to avoid fighting altogether. Political objectives and the ways they are affected by the successes and failures of combat are for Clausewitz of utmost importance. Sun Zi assumes a straightforward political goal. After this goal has been conveyed to him by the ruler, the general does what is appropriate until he wins. The reciprocal interaction between politics and fighting, upon which Clausewitz lays such stress, is virtually absent in Sun Zi. "The peculiar nature of its means" is what distinguishes war from other forms of political activity according to Clausewitz, who discusses much about war other than its means. Methods, however, "Soldierly Methods," are Sun Zi's primary and almost sole concern.

For both authors, the goal of war is, as Clausewitz states it, "to compel the enemy to do our will."[7] But how is this to be done? Clausewitz assumes the task will be accomplished by "an act of force."[8] The use of force is, after all, the feature that Clausewitz takes as distinguishing war from other state activities, such as diplomacy. But Sun Zi, concerned not with war so much as with the methods best employed by soldiers, seeks to minimize the use of force, rather as did the mercenary leaders, the *condottieri* of the European renaissance.

Probably the most celebrated and often quoted line from Sun Zi is the one that Professor Mair renders as: "Being victorious a hundred times in a hundred battles is not the most excellent approach. Causing the enemy forces to submit without a battle is the most excellent approach."[9] The vision of victory without fighting is fundamental to Sun Zi's entire argument. I will turn in a moment to considering how he seeks to achieve it. But his search for victory without what Clausewitz regularly calls "the maximum use of force"[10] is evident simply from the low frequency with which Sun Zi invokes the concept. The Chinese word *li* 力, meaning "force," is used only nine times in all thirteen chapters of Sun Zi, with some of these occurrences being negative in implication, in fact, warnings against the misuse of force. The corresponding German word, *Gewalt*, by contrast occurs eight times in *just the two paragraphs* in which Clausewitz defines war.[11]

Clausewitz could not be clearer in his insistence that fighting is at the center of warfare. As he puts it in a celebrated passage:

> We are not interested in generals who win victories without bloodshed. The fact that slaughter is a horrifying spectacle must make us take war more seriously, but not provide an excuse for gradually blunting our swords in the name of humanity. Sooner or later someone will come along with a sharp sword and hack off our arms.[12]

What, then, is Clausewitz's *soldierly method*? It is, to be sure, to wage war ferociously, exerting maximum force, but in a carefully considered way. But the mind is key to how force is to be applied. "The maximum use of force is in no way incompatible with the simultaneous use of the intellect."[13] As the shape of the conflict becomes clear, the perceptive general will be able to identify what Clausewitz calls the "center of gravity [*Schwerpunkt*]." As he explains, "One must keep the dominant characteristics of both belligerents in mind. Out of those characteristics a certain *center of gravity* develops, the hub of all power and movement, on which everything depends. That is the point at which all our energies should be directed."[14] This center of gravity is likely to be military: the army of the opposing commander, for example. But it need not be such. Clausewitz is fully aware that some other aspect of a society at war may be all important and potentially decisive.

For Alexander, Gustavus Adolphus, Charles XII, and Frederick the Great, the center of gravity was their army. If the army had been destroyed, they would all have gone down in history as failures. In countries subject to domestic strife, the center of gravity is generally the capital. In small countries that rely on large ones, it is usually the army of their protector. Among alliances, it lies in the community of interest, and in popular uprisings it is the personalities of the leaders and public opinion. It is against these that our energies should be directed. If the enemy is thrown off balance, he must not be given time to recover. Blow after blow must be aimed in the same direction: the victor, in other words, must strike with all his strength, and not just against a fraction of the enemy's. Not by taking things the easy way—using superior strength to filch some province, preferring the security of this minor conquest to great success—but by constantly seeking out the center of his power, and by daring all to win all, will one really defeat the enemy.[15]

Sun Zi adopts a different premise. Far from finding the center of gravity in the battle, he finds it in the psychology of the adversary. His goal is to unnerve his opponents, to demoralize them, to mislead them, and to outmaneuver and threaten them, in such a way that their social cohesion breaks down and their rulers and military find themselves in disorder and chaos. If force is indispensable to doing this then he advocates its careful use. But he does not look to force as a first resort.

The chaos and disorder Sun Zi seeks to create may be a physical state resulting from a decisive military defeat. But its sources are psychological. A useful way of understanding this is to say that while Clausewitz seeks to take a state that is independent and defiant, and inflict upon it physical and moral defeat, Sun Zi seeks to undermine the orderliness of his opponent, the situation expressed by the character *zhi* 治, in which the state is being stably ruled, and render it *luan* 亂, which is to say, chaotic. The Chinese populations for control of which the kings of the warring states contended had no nationalistic passions of the sort that enflamed the Napoleonic Wars. Provided rule was not too onerous, they cared no more about which kingly clan was in charge than did German farmers in the Holy Roman Empire about which of a changeable constellation of nobles and ecclesiastical authorities had sovereignty over them. With Sun Zi we are in a world that corresponds to the European world of dynasties, in which kings fought with specialized armies and ordinary people cared little about the outcome of war. Clausewitz writes about quite a different world, most importantly, one in which national identities are congealing and national passions have been released.

For Sun Zi, then, the center of gravity is not the enemy's army or his capital. It is the enemy's mind and the morale of his soldiers. How, we may ask, does Sun Zi suggest we attack such an intangible-seeming a target?

Sun Zi's method can be summed up by four characters, in sequence. These are *quan* 權, which we may call "assessment" (the word's origin is "to weigh"); *shi* 勢, which should be understood as all of the factors and tendencies bearing on a possible battle, and which Mair translates marvelously as "configuration"; then *ji* 幾, which indicates the moment at which the "configuration" of the various influences is most propitious for action; and finally *mou* 謀, which is often translated by the little-used English word "stratagem," a term that suggests not simply an "operational plan" as it would be called today, but in particular an operational plan that extracts maximum value from psychological as opposed to material factors. An ambush is a stratagem; a frontal attack is simply an operational plan.

Clausewitz would probably agree with all of this, except for the implication that if properly executed—indeed, if properly threatened but *not* executed—the method Sun Zi proposes can transform order or *zhi* into chaos or *luan* simply by psychological dislocation.

Certainly the great Prussian writer would agree about the tremendous importance of judgment, *quan*. This is apparent in the stress he lays on the quality and independent creativity of the commander, to whom he accords every bit as much importance as does Sun Zi. For it is from the mind of the commander that victory comes. Material balances, morale, logistics, and so forth are all important. But only a commander of genius can develop a winning strategy or stratagem. Both authors, therefore, differ very much from writers who see warfare as a test of national resources, technology, and resolve. War is above all a matter of solving complex intellectual problems, many of which have no simple formula or algorithm. Sun Zi would agree, I think, with Clausewitz that:

> The man responsible for evaluating the whole must bring to his task the quality of intuition that perceives the truth at every point. . . . Bonaparte rightly said in this connection that many of the decisions faced by the commander-in-chief resemble mathematical problems worthy of the gifts of a *Newton* or an *Euler*.
>
> What this task requires in the way of higher intellectual gifts is a sense of unity and a power of judgment raised to a marvelous pitch of vision, which easily grasps and dismisses a thousand remote possibilities which an ordinary mind would labor to identify and wear itself out in so doing.[16]

Where the two men would disagree, I think, is about the means that the commander of genius will employ. How does Sun Zi envision decisive psychological dislocation as being achieved absent the use of force?

In a famous passage, Sun Zi writes that all war is deception, *gui dao* 詭道. When Westerners think of deception their minds will likely turn to dummy tanks and guns or, at the best, to the successful allied effort to mislead the Germans as to where the D-Day landing would occur. No Western strategist, and certainly not Clausewitz, would ever put deception at the heart of military method. Yet Sun Zi does this. The fact is clear linguistically. In Chinese philosophy, the moral way, or *dao* 道, is what gives rulers their legitimacy and society its cohesion. Sun Zi makes this clear at the very beginning of his treatise. The centrality of the concept in general political thought means that its manipulation must also be central. To twist the *dao* itself and create a deceptive *dao* is to subvert the foundation upon which all society and human activity is believed, by Chinese philosophers, to rest. Doing so is therefore far more grave and potentially far more powerful than any mere "deception" would be in the West.

Western writers and strategists have understood the importance of psychological dimensions in warfare. Consider the climax of the Battle of Waterloo. As John Keegan describes it:

> Napoleon was heavily engaged on two fronts and threatened with encirclement by the advancing Prussians. He had only one group of soldiers left with which to break the closing ring and swing the advantage back to himself. This group was the infantry of the Imperial Guard. At about seven it left its position. . . . The British battalions on the crest fired volleys into its front and flank . . . heavy *and unexpected* [emphasis supplied]—and, to their surprise, saw the Guard turn and disappear into the smoke from which it had emerged. On the Duke of Wellington's signal, the whole line advanced. . . . Napoleon had been beaten.[17]

The sudden turn of the tide caused by the withdrawal of *La Garde* fits into a Western pattern of warfare that has existed since the hoplite battles in Greek times, in which the final phase of "collapse" or *trope* (τροπη) is followed by "confusion, misdirection, and mob violence."[18] At Waterloo, just why the Imperial Guard pulled back is impossible to say, but Keegan and others stress psychological factors.[19]

But as we will see, Western methods of war have evolved away from psychological means toward ever greater applications of men, technology, and materiel. At Waterloo the retreat of the Guards took all by surprise. Chinese operations, by contrast, invariably have a strong psychological aspect even today. Perhaps the best example is the collapse of the Eighth Army in Korea, which led to the longest retreat in American military history and introduced the phrase "bug out" to our language. This began in late November 1950, as American forces approached the Yalu River, when Chinese units that had been secretly deployed outflanked and ambushed the American Second Division at the disastrous battle of Kunu-ri beginning November 26. In the period that followed, morale collapsed, and most of the Americans fled in disorder.[20] Chaos and disorder induced by psychological mechanisms triggered by military facts have a long history in both China and the West.

In the Bible we learn that the Philistines were thrown into disorder when they realized that no less than Yahweh himself was assisting the Israelites in I Samuel 7:10. "The Philistines drew near to battle against Israel: but the LORD thundered with a great thunder on that day upon the Philistines and discomfited them; and they were smitten before Israel." Here "discomfited" is the Hebrew "*wayehummem* [וַיְהֻמֵּם]," meaning "to throw into confusion and panic" and is used especially with Yahweh as subject and an enemy as object within a holy war context. The associated noun *mehumah* [מְהוּמָה] denotes "the divine consternation or panic" produced by Yahweh's self-manifestation, through storms.[21]

The Canaanite god Ba'al was also well known "as the divine warrior and thunderer." According to Frank Cross, one pattern of such appearance is "the march of the Divine Warrior to battle, bearing his terrible weapons, the thunder-bolt and the winds. He

drives his fiery cloud-chariot against his enemy. His wrath is reflected in all nature. Mountains shatter; the heavens collapse at his
glance. A terrible slaughter is appointed."[22]

As Jeffrey Tigay points out (see note 21), a similar notion of
decisive confusion in war is conveyed by the Greek *kudoimos*
(κυδοιμοσ), as in the *Iliad,* when Athena intervenes:

There he [Achilles] stood, and shouted, and from her place
    Pallas Athene
Gave cry, and drove an endless terror [i.e., confusion] upon
    the Trojans.[23]

Or the comparable phenomenon in the *Odyssey,* as the long-absent
hero slays his wife's suitors:

And now Athene waved the aegis [shield] that blights
    humanity,
from high aloft on the roof, and all their wits were
    bewildered;
and they stampeded about the hall, like a herd of cattle
set upon and driven wild by the darting horsefly.[24]

Tian 天, the Chinese "Heaven," lacked the anthropomorphic
features of the Yahweh or Ba'al or Pallas Athena, but it could inter-
vene in battle, through the power of virtue, or *de* 德.

For Confucian thinkers, a ruler who followed the way of the
true king (*wang dao* 王道) would never need to use force. His
moral example would be enough to give order to his realm.
The proof text is the classical account of how the Zhou dynasty
overthrew the corrupt Shang at the semilegendary battle of the
Wilderness of Mu [*Muye*] 牧野] in 1045 B.C., which Confucian
philosophers took as the prototype of proper warfare. According
to the *Classic of Documents,* the Shang troops "would offer no

opposition to our army. Those in front inverted their spears and attacked those behind them, till they fled, and the blood flowed." The victory was achieved by the working of Zhou virtue on the Shang forces. The empire was restored in the same way: King Wu of Zhou "had only to let his robes fall down, and fold his hands, and the empire was orderly ruled."[25]

Sun Zi, to be sure, does not rely upon Heaven to produce the psychological dislocation that brings the enemy down. Nor does he look for repeated military blows to produce it. Instead, Sun Zi *assumes that he will possess near-perfect knowledge of the enemy's dispositions*—intelligence dominance in today's parlance—as well as secret agents in the enemy's country and even his court, ready to rise up when the signal is given. He will be able to deceive his adversary and move unobserved. (His own dispositions, however, will be utterly opaque to the enemy.) When the enemy discovers the hopelessness of its situation, its commander will find himself totally bewildered, and its troops will panic. Divine intervention is not necessary for this. "Betrayal" is enough, as in the French cry, "*Nous sommes trahis!* [We are betrayed!]," often heard when they have, in fact, simply been outmaneuvered, or the simple "We're buggin' out—We're movin' on!" of the Second Division's "Bugout Boogie."[26]

Clausewitz understands psychological factors, but he does not believe they can reliably stand alone or play a greater role in battle than actual fighting. As for intelligence, on the basis of his many years as a soldier, Clausewitz simply discounts the possibility of ever achieving such dominance as Sun Zi takes for granted. Clausewitz is dismissive about intelligence in general:

> The textbooks agree, of course, that we should only believe reliable intelligence, and should never cease to be suspicious, but what is the use of such feeble maxims? They belong to that

wisdom which for want of anything better scribblers of systems and compendia resort to when they run out of ideas. Many intelligence reports in war are contradictory, even more are false, and most are uncertain.[27]

Here in fact is the basic difference between Clausewitz and Sun Zi. Perhaps because he lives in a culturally uniform world having very limited resources, Sun Zi concentrates on making the most of nonmaterial cultural commonalities (which render deception and espionage easier) and minimizing the expenditure of materiel. Clausewitz lives in a world where nation-states are very different, espionage and deception difficult, and materiel relatively more abundant. In any case, Sun Zi is above all concerned with maximizing the efficacy of any military operation while limiting its duration. Indeed, the duration of his ideal military operation, which succeeds without fighting, is zero. Clausewitz, by contrast, seeks to maximize the cumulative effectiveness of force applied over time, against the enemy's center of gravity.

What we have here are two different approaches to the problem of the great costliness of war. In the West conflicts were often over matters difficult to resolve, such as religious belief or national affiliation, and even the most skillful military tactics—Napoleon's for example—could not avoid immense costs. So the *state was transformed* in the West to support such war: serfdom was abolished; taxation and national borrowing greatly expanded; armies were reformed and made professional; national leadership was entrenched and legitimized by mass participation; and so forth. In China, however, the goal was usually control of a people left unchanged by the conflict, and the attempt was to *transform war* so as to make it less costly and more rapidly decisive. This is what the Chinese military classics are about.

Consider Sun Zi's idea of "configuration." What this means is that, over time, day to day or hour to hour, the potential effectiveness of a military operation will rise and fall as the factors contributing to configuration change. Sun Zi has only a limited amount of force at his disposal. Once it has fought, his army cannot be replenished to fight again. So configuration must be assessed with great precision, and the moment to expend force must be chosen with care. The natural and other forces associated with war are far more powerful than any military factors. Compared to the number of opportunities presented, Sun Zi's general will fight only rarely.

Clausewitz, by contrast, expects war to go on until one side or the other is broken: materially, strategically, psychologically, or all three. Many factors may slow war down. At some point only the will of the commander remains. But persistence in fighting, provided strategy and tactics are sound, is likely to prevail—but cumulatively, not instantaneously.

Now suppose that we think about this using the language of mathematics. Suppose we graph the potential effectiveness of a military operation, expressing it as $y = f(x)$ where x is time and y is the effectiveness of a military operation, with $f(x)$ being a measurement or a function that processes all the factors bearing on "configuration" and their interactions at time x.

In other words, if c represents the weighted value of one or another dimension of "configuration" at time x, $f(x)$ may be thought of as $\Sigma\ c_1 + c_2 + \ldots c_n$ where n is the number of variables being considered. What aspects of this curve will be of interest to Sun Zi? The answer, I think, is that Sun Zi will be most interested in the points where the curve changes direction or reaches a maximum or minimum, that is to say, in f' and f'', the first and second derivatives of the function.

What will Clausewitz be interested in? For him, military effort is continuous, so he will want to look at the sum total, the cumulation of the function, over a period of time, that is, the area under the curve. In mathematical terms, if x is time, it is the integral from $x = 0$ to $x = t$ of the function, i.e., $\int_0^t f(x)$.

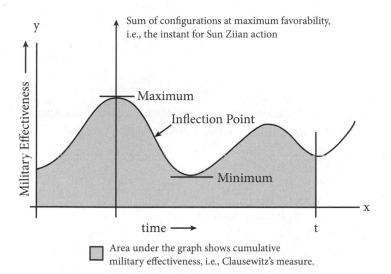

Area under the graph shows cumulative military effectiveness, i.e., Clausewitz's measure.

Of course, it would be absurd to attempt to quantify Clausewitz or Sun Zi. Both stress the independence of mind that goes into inventing good stratagems and making wise choices. The point of using mathematical language here is to drive home the basic difference between the two thinkers that I have attempted to state above in ordinary English. Clausewitz is an "integral strategist," concerned with prolongation of effort, the summing up of various components of a strategy at a culminating point—the entire area under the curve. Sun Zi is what might be called a "differential strategist," concerned with timing, turning points, and the ever-changing play of circumstances and opportunities. His ideal war is one in which the fighting diminishes to zero: in other words, in which the short and decisive battle reaches its limit, as an infinitesimal.

The phenomenon they examine is the same. But their approaches are both mutually exclusive and mutually necessary for completeness, just as differentiation and integration are in mathematics.

Bryn Mawr, Pennsylvania
January 2007

Notes

1. Carl von Clausewitz, *On War*, trans. Michael Howard and Peter Paret (Princeton, N.J.: Princeton University Press, 1976; indexed edition, 1984).
2. Clausewitz, *On War*, p. 5.
3. Clausewitz, *On War*, p. 77 (1.1.3).
4. Clausewitz, *On War*, p. 79 (1.1.8).
5. Clausewitz, *On War*, p. 80 (1.1.9).
6. Clausewitz, *On War*, p. 87 (1.1.24), emphasis supplied.
7. Clausewitz, *On War*, p. 75 (1.1.2).
8. Clausewitz, *On War*, p. 75 (1.1.2).
9. See chapter 3, p. 85.
10. E.g., Clausewitz, *On War*, p. 76 (1.1.3).
11. Clausewitz, *On War*, p. 75 (1.1.2).
12. Clausewitz, *On War*, p. 260 (4.11).
13. Clausewitz, *On War*, p. 75 (1.1.3).
14. Clausewitz, *On War*, pp. 595–96 (8.4).
15. Clausewitz, *On War*, p. 596 (8.4).
16. Clausewitz, *On War*, p. 112 (1.3).
17. John Keegan, *The Face of Battle* (New York: The Viking Press, 1976), p. 127.
18. Victor Davis Hanson, *The Western Way of War: Infantry Battle in Classical Greece* (Berkeley: University of California Press, 1989), pp. 185–93.
19. Keegan, *Face of Battle*, pp. 177 ff.
20. See T. R. Fehrenbach, *This Kind of War* (1963; Washington, D.C.: Brassey's, 1998), pp. 202 ff.

21. King James Version. See William Foxwell Albright and David Noel Freedman, gen. eds., *The Anchor Bible*, vol. 8, *I Samuel*, trans., intro., notes, and commentary by P. Kyle McCarter Jr. (Garden City, N.Y.: Doubleday & Co., Inc., 1980), pp. 106n. 5, 145n. 10. For definitive discussion of the Hebrew terms, see *The JPS Torah Commentary: Deuteronomy: The Traditional Hebrew Text with the New JPS Translation*, with commentary by Jeffrey Tigay (Philadelphia: The Jewish Publication Society, 1996), on Deuteronomy 2:14, which notes, "The noun *mehumah* means 'confusion,' 'turmoil,' 'tumult.' It is used in reference to war, to confusion that can cause soldiers to kill their comrades, to the pandemonium caused by a raging pestilence, and to social disorder. Here it is comparable to the [Greek] *kudoimos*, κυδοιμοσ, the confusion or tumult (sometimes personified) that the gods inflict on the enemies of their protégés in the Homeric epics."

22. Frank Moore Cross, *Canaanite Myth and Hebrew Epic: Essays in the History of the Religion of Israel* (Cambridge, Mass.: Harvard University Press, 1973), pp. 150, 155–56.

23. *Iliad* 18:217–18, trans. Richmond Lattimore (Chicago: University of Chicago Press, 1951), p. 381; cited in Tigay, *The JPS Torah Commentary: Deuteronomy*.

24. *Odyssey* 22:297–300, trans. Richmond Lattimore (New York: Harper Perennial, 1991), p. 331; cited in Tigay, *The JPS Torah Commentary: Deuteronomy*.

25. *Shujing* 5.3.9–10; see "The Shoo King," in *The Chinese Classics*, trans. James Legge, reprint ed. (Taipei: Wen Shi Zhe, 1971), 3:315–16.

26. Fehrenbach, *This Kind of War*, p. 202.

27. Clausewitz, *On War*, p. 117 (1.6.117).

It was Jennifer Crewe, editorial director at Columbia University Press, who suggested that I do a translation of Sun Zi's *Art of War*. This was not an undertaking that I ever would have thought of on my own. Once I embarked on it, however, I began to realize its importance, and my investigations into the history and nature of the *Sun Zi* became an enjoyable and compelling task. I carried out most of my research on the text during the years 2003 and 2004, but the actual translation was done entirely during the period from August 14 to September 7, 2005, while I was traveling from Philadelphia to Hong Kong, Changchun, Ji'an, Shanghai, Beijing, Bombay, Hyderabad, and then back to Philadelphia to meet with various colleagues and to attend a series of conferences. As I often tell my friends and students, a lot of my most creative and productive work is done in the sky, at an altitude of 35,000 feet.

I should have finished this volume back in 2004 at the latest, but my teaching duties and a host of unexpected obligations intervened. Despite the long delay, Ms. Crewe was extraordinarily patient and understanding, which has been a source of much-needed encouragement in a time of great personal difficulties.

Consequently, I wish to express my deep gratitude to her for helping me bring this long project to completion.

As with all of my research, the librarians at the University of Pennsylvania have contributed greatly to the making of this volume. I am particularly indebted to Jidong Yang, Alban Kojima, and Julianna Lipschutz for assisting me in tracking down books, articles, and Web resources that were essential for completing this translation and study.

Four long-term, long-distance correspondents—Carol Conti-Entin, Julie Lee Wei, Mineda McCleave, and Justine Snow—have been a source of inspiration and information. I thank each of them for their critical acumen and warm understanding. I am equally indebted to all of my wonderful, brilliant students, both those in the past and those in the present. To one extent or another, everything that I write has been shaped by the close intellectual experiences that I have shared with them. No professor has ever been blessed with a better cohort of undergraduate and graduate students than I. Without in any way wanting to slight any of the others, here I shall mention by name only Ahmad Bashi (an Iraqi genius), with whom I had the pleasure of reading through the entire *Sun Zi* in a one-on-one tutorial a couple of years ago. Ahmad's insights were of great help in getting at the deeper levels of significance in the text.

Another genius who has contributed to the making of this book is Daniel Heitkamp, creator of the magnificent woodcuts that grace the title and dedication pages. I consider myself tremendously fortunate to be able to cooperate with an artist who can take my rough ideas and turn them into something sublime.

Naturally, I owe much to the many scholars around the world who have studied the *Sun Zi* and related texts. In a more general way, I feel a deep sense of gratitude to all the Sinologists who have shaped our field, making participation in it a rigorously professional privilege. I would like to single out one individual in particular who has done as much as anyone to define Sinology for our times, in the process saving my colleagues and me countless hours in our research. That is Endymion Wilkinson, former ambassador of the European Union to the People's Republic of China, who authored *Chinese History: A Manual* (2000). For the present volume, Wilkinson's chapter 28, "War" (pp. 554–64) has been of inestimable value, but it is simply mind-boggling that his *Manual* has equally valuable chapters on virtually all other aspects of Chinese civilization and culture. Never mind that he is now bringing to completion the third revised and enlarged edition of this mammoth treasury, nor that he even does the typesetting himself; it is enough just to ramble joyfully through the pages of the *Manual* without trying to comprehend how it was created by one man.

So many others have contributed to the making of this book that it would be difficult for me to name them all. Among those whom I would certainly not want to miss are Mark Edward Lewis (military history); Mark Swofford (grammatical analysis and Internet resources [William Hannas, Michael Carr, David Moser, and Ivan Aymat also helped in the latter regard]); Elfriede Regina Knauer, Georg Knauer, Joseph Farrell, Ralph Rosen, Jeremy McInerney, Charles Kahn, and Adrienne Mayor (Greek and Roman materials); Ludo Rocher and Lars Martin Fosse (Sanskrit literature); H[oong] T[eik] Toh (Manchu and Tangut translations); Sanping Chen (Inner Asian history); Milan Hejtmanek (Korean history); James P. Mallory (archeology); Calvert Watkins, Donald Ringe, and Douglas Adams (Indo-European linguistics); Bill Darden (Slavic linguistics); Michael Witzel, Harold C. Fleming, Václav Blažek, and John D. Bengtson (Afro-Asiatic linguistics); Laurent Sagart, Axel Schuessler, W. South Coblin, and David Prager Branner (Sinitic linguistics), David A. Graff, Peter Lorge, Steve Tinney, Jeffrey Tigay, Joseph Lowry, and Barry Eichler (ancient weapons); Edward Tenner, Emma Bunker, Karen Rubinson, Gunar Freibergs, and Ulf Jäger (ancient armor); E. Bruce Brooks (composition

of the *Sun Zi* and other early Chinese texts); Roger Ames and
Ralph Sawyer (manuscripts of the *Sun Zi* and the *Sun Bin bingfa*);
Anthony Diller (astronomical and calendrical systems); Gavin
LaRowe and Donald B. Wagner (iron technology); Robin D. S.
Yates (the *Mo Zi* and siegecraft); William H. Nienhauser Jr. (the
Shi ji); W. Allyn Rickett (the *Guan Zi*); Paul R. Goldin (the *Xun Zi*
and other Han and earlier texts); Jens Østergård Petersen (genealogy of "Sun Wu"); Eric Henry (pre-Qin cultural history); David
Anthony (horses and chariots); Ruth Meserve (Inner Asian animal
lore); Meir Shahar (martial arts); Joshua Capitanio (martial arts
and Taoism); David W. Goodrich and Fang Shizeng (typesetting
and computing); Stephen F. Teiser (for sending me essential books
from Princeton); Stefan Krasowski and Xu Wenkan (for sending
vital materials from China); Arthur Waldron (for writing the foreword); and Philip Miraglia (for keeping my computers healthy). I
have also benefited from close readings of an earlier version of the
manuscript by two anonymous reviewers for Columbia University
Press who offered many valuable suggestions for improvement.

It is clear from the different fields of expertise mentioned in
the preceding paragraph that my research on the *Sun Zi bingfa*
encompassed a far broader range and greater depth than may be
evident from the book itself. Although by no means did everything that I learned in the process of preparing this volume end up
being incorporated in it, I believe that the knowledge I absorbed
during the last three years has contributed to making this work
more reliable and insightful than it might otherwise have been.
Furthermore, I may eventually write a series of short papers on
various related topics, such as the early evolution of the concept of
fa ("law, method") in China, the identification of the *qilin* (Japanese *kirin;* **not** "unicorn"), Eurasian words for weapons, metals,
and horses, and so forth. If that should transpire, then I would
be doubly indebted to those who have been so generous while I
was writing the present work. I wish to make clear, however, that

I alone am responsible for the entirety of the content and expression of all publications that appear under my name, including this volume.

Appreciation is also due to my son, Thomas Krishna, and my brother, Thomas Lee, for numerous favors. They took care of many important tasks (such as tracking down and purchasing things on the Web) that I am incapable of myself.

Last, but certainly not least, I would like to thank my *taitai*, Li-ching, for her willingness to listen patiently (most of the time) to my endless babbling over Sun Zi and all manner of other scholarly obsessions. Not only did she listen, she also offered constructive (and sometimes pointed) criticism, which has contributed immeasurably to the quality of all the work I have done for the last three decades and more.

Swarthmore, Pennsylvania

August 15, 2006

Note: This translation, together with its introduction and notes, is intended to be fully accessible to the nonspecialist. Specialists who want a more detailed treatment of topics that are touched upon here, including more densely philological treatment of specific terms, may consult the author's "*Soldierly Methods:* Introduction and Notes for an Iconoclastic Translation of *Sun Zi bingfa,*" which is available on the Web as *Sino-Platonic Papers* 178 (February 2008).

The *Sun Zi* is written in a style that is often highly abbreviated and elliptical. Both the subject and the object, as well as other parts of the sentence, may be omitted, and even whole clauses may be dispensed with. One may think of this style as telegraphic (or, in current terms, written as though for purposes of short text messaging [STM]), at times carried to an extreme, making the text extraordinarily terse and maddeningly obscure. Since all of these missing elements are essential in normal English both for grammatical reasons and for the reader to gain a full understanding of the purport of the Chinese text, I have silently added a word or two here and there. Occasionally, however, when I have provided intratextual amplification or clarification that exceeds more than two or three words, I generally signal these longer or more substantial additions in a note.

The chief principles adhered to in this translation are the following:

I. *Being overly literal does not necessarily ensure accuracy.* A frequently recurring expression in the *Sun Zi* is *yong bing*. Literally, in the narrowest, most primitive sense, it signifies "use weapon(s)." However, it never means that in the *Sun Zi*. Instead, it conveys the idea of "employ soldiers," "conduct military operations," "engage in warfare," or "wage war" (I consistently render *yong bing* with the last English equivalent).

II. *Do not be too free.* This is the opposite of the previous principle. One of the most important terms for nearly all schools of early Chinese thought is *dao* ("way"; Mair 1990:132–33; Zhang 2002:11–26). For obviously ulterior purposes, some modern interpreters render *dao* as "God," distorting the term so horrendously as to make it impossible to understand the ideas presented in the original texts where it occurs.

III. *Be consistent, but not mechanically so.* The same word in a given text may mean two or more very different things. For example, in the *Sun Zi, xing* can signify both "form(ation)" and "type (of terrain)." If one fails to distinguish the distinction between these two vital concepts, it would be impossible to make sense of the arguments that are put forward in the text. On the other hand, when the same term always conveys an identical meaning, there is no reason not to be consistent in the way one renders it, and there are many advantages to doing so. For instance, a characteristic structural feature of the *Sun Zi* is that its maxims are frequently loosely linked by the conjunction *gu* ("therefore"). Many translators, fearing that the monotony of this usage might lead to boredom, vary their renderings of *gu* as "hence," "thus," and so forth. In my estimation, by so doing they fail to convey to their readers both the rhetorical flavor and stylistic quality of the original text.

IV. *Strive to convey a sense of the form and essence of the original.* When one is reading a translation, one should be at least subliminally aware that one is encountering a text from another language and another culture, both of which have distinctive, quintessential features. To reduce them to something that is identical with an original text written in English is tantamount to having failed to convey the essential quality of the work being translated. This is not, however, to advocate exoticization, chinoiserie, or other such clumsy crudities. Rather, I believe that the translator should simply respect the text that he has undertaken to present in another language, and that he should do his utmost to honor its inmost nature.

V. *A translation should be readable without recourse to notes or other supplementary material.* The present translation is accompanied by an extensive introduction, numerous annotations, an appendix, and other supplementary materials. These are intended purely for enrichment and enhancement and to satisfy the curiosity of those who wish to go beyond the experience of reading the translation itself. No one should feel obliged to read all of the introductory and commentarial apparatus. For this policy to succeed, however, it is necessary to make slight adjustments and amplifications in the translation itself, so that there are no portions of it that remain opaque to the neophyte. When such adjustments and amplifications are significant, however, they should be signaled so that fidelity can be maintained.

The base text for this translation is *Song ben shiyi jia zhu Sun Zi* (Song edition of the *Sun Zi* with annotations by eleven commentators) (Zhonghua shuju Shanghai editorial office, 1961) as presented in *Sun Zi bingfa xinzhu* (*Master Sun's Military Methods,* newly annotated) (for complete publication information see under Zhongguo Renmin Jiefang Jun in the bibliography). The *Sun Zi bingfa xinzhu* has been reprinted numerous times since the first edition of 1977, with well over half a million copies having been issued. This is an extremely handy edition of the *Sun Zi,* since it provides a reliable base text, significant variants (including those from recently discovered manuscripts), and a judicious combination of ancient and modern annotations, together with general discussions of the contents of each chapter. Two appendices are the so-called biography of Master Sun from *Shi ji* (*The Grand Scribe's Records*) and the carefully edited bamboo-strip manuscript of the *Sun Zi* in thirteen fragmentary chapters (only the title of the tenth chapter survives), plus five other fragmentary chapters that are thought to be closely associated with the *Sun Zi* (three of the texts do mention a Master Sun [the first, the third, and the fifth], and two of them [the first and the last] also mention the king of Wu [specifically He Lu in the latter case], and it is possible that they are meant to be from the hand of the legendary Sun Wu). I have also consulted dozens of other commentaries, some of which are mentioned in the introduction or are listed in the bibliography.

The standard system of transcription for Chinese characters in this book is Modern Standard Mandarin (MSM), as represented in *pinyin* (the official romanization of the People's Republic of China). This is purely a convention of modern scholarship and does not at all reflect the pronunciation of Sinitic during the late Warring States period when this text was compiled. Transcribing Chinese characters into Cantonese or Taiwanese would actually be preferable, in the sense of sounding more like ancient Sinitic, since—of all modern Chinese languages and topolects—MSM has diverged the furthest from ancient and medieval pronunciations. Unfortunately, the field has not yet reached that stage.

Vowels

In MSM vowels are generally long, as in many continental (European) languages; thus:

>   *a* is pronounced as in "father," not as in "matter"
>   *i* is pronounced as the "ee" of "beet" or "peek," but after *z, c, s,*

zh, ch, sh, and r (for which, see below) it is pronounced like the "i" of "bit"

u is pronounced as the "oo" of "boo!" except after q and x, when it is pronounced like ü (see below)

e and o are a bit more difficult to grasp, with e sounding somewhat like the "u" of "lucky" and o sounding roughly like the "o" of "more"

ü sounds like the same umlauted letter in German, comparable to "you"

DIPHTHONGS

ao sounds like "ow!"

iu sounds like "yo!"

ai sounds like "eye"

ei sounds like the letter "a"

ou sounds like the letter "o"

uo or wo sounds like the combination of pinyin w and o

CONSONANTS

Most of the consonants in pinyinized MSM sound more or less like their counterparts in English, with the following exceptions:

c sounds like the "ts" of "tsetse fly"; thus "Cao Cao" is pronounced not as "cow cow," but as "Ts'ao Ts'ao," with noticeable aspiration

j sounds like the "g" of "gee"

x sounds like the "sh" of "she"

q sounds like the "ch" of "cheese"

z sounds like the "dz" of "adze"

ch sounds like the "ch" of "chintz" or "change"

sh sounds like the "sh" or "shin" or "shame"

zh sounds like the "g" of "gip / gyp" or the "j" of "jam"

r has a slight buzzing aspect to it, as though one were trying to pronounce "r" and "zz" (lightly) at the same time

TONES

Sinitic languages are tonal, and MSM is no different, having four tones plus a neutral tone (i.e., the absence of the other four tones). It is too much to ask noninitiates to cope with the tones when they already have so much to do in dealing with the vowels and consonants, some of which are quite counterintuitive for speakers of English. However, without the tones, homonyms sometimes occur. In order to differentiate them, I have marked the vowels of the relevant syllables with tonal diacritics when they are otherwise identical (e.g., *jī* and *jì, qí* and *qì*).

EXAMPLE

Following these rules, when we pronounce the title of this work, Sun Zi sounds like "Soon Dz," *bing* sounds like a kind of luscious dark cherry, and *fa* sounds like a note to follow do, re, mi: *Soon Dz bingfa.*

Here are highlighted only several of the more important words and subtle concepts used in the book. Other technical terms and proper nouns are defined in the notes or in the introduction. For a superb handbook of basic Chinese philosophical terms, including many that are featured in the *Sun Zi*, see Zhang Dainian, *Key Concepts in Chinese Philosophy*, trans. Edmund Ryden.

BIAN. Variation, variety, transformation.

BING. The earliest form of the character used to write this word depicts two arms holding up an adze. The basic idea conveyed by this graph subsequently developed from the concrete and limited to the more general and abstract: weapon → soldier → troops → war.

FA. Law, method, model.

BINGFA. The combination of the previous two terms, it is usually rendered as "art of war" in English but may more literally be rendered as "soldierly methods," "military methods," etc. For further discussion of *bingfa*, see the introduction, n. 2.

GUI. Deceit, deception; something contrary to the norm.

JĪ. Pivot, moment of change (functions somewhat like a tipping point); the instant just before a new development or shift occurs; the nodal point of a situation in flux. *Jī* also refers to the first, imperceptible beginning of movement in an unstable situation. In organic metaphors, it means "seed, germ." The sage or superior man can recognize the immanence or incipience of these crucial moments before they become manifest to others. It cannot be stressed too heavily that *jī* by itself does not mean "opportunity" nor does it mean "crisis," although it is closer to the latter than to the former because of the extreme instability of a given situation and the unforeseen consequences that may follow.

JÌ. Count, calculate; plan; intention. Another word in the *Sun Zi* sometimes rendered as "plan" is *mou* (as in the title of chap. 3), though it tends more in the direction of "scheme" or "counsel." Depending upon the context, *jì* and *mou* may also convey the idea of "strategy" or "stratagem."

LǏ. A traditional measure of length equivalent to 300 paces (hence "tricent" in English). It is easy to think of how long a tricent is (about a third of a mile) by recalling that the English word "mile" is derived from Latin *milia, millia* ("a thousand [paces]"). For those who are not familiar with miles, a tricent is equal to approximately half a kilometer.

LÌ. Advantage, benefit; profit, interest (the basic meaning is "sharp," which is why the character used to write it has a "knife" radical).

MOU. See *jì*.

QÌ. Unformed, energetic substrate of matter; material energy; the primal "stuff" of the universe; configural energy. In the *Sun Zi*, it usually refers to the vital force, energy, or morale of the men in the army. For more information on *qì* and its metaphysical implications, see Mair (1990:137–38) and Zhang (2002:45–63).

QÍ. See *zheng*

QUAN. Power, expedient (assessment)—exerted by the commander in the field. The literal meaning of the morpheme is "horizontal balance," hence "weigh, judge, (exert) power/authority." *Quan* is often associated with *bian* or *qí* (qq.v.).

SHI. Configuration, circumstances, efficacy, inertia, power/force (of circumstances), authority, (strategic/positional) advantage. The subject of chap. 5, but also discussed elsewhere in the text, this is one of the key concepts of the *Sun Zi*. It is also one of the most ineffable.

TIANXIA. All under heaven, i.e., the empire (writ large).

WEN. Civil, culture (contrasts with *wu*). The evolution of the primary meanings of the graph used to write this word, in simplest terms, is as follows: tattoo → pattern → culture/civilization/writing. The earliest meaning of *wen* as "tattoo" still survives in the expression *wen shen* ("tattoo the body"). By the time of the Warring States period, however, when the *Sun Zi* was written, tattooing had become a form of punishment, and different words were used to refer to it, *wen* itself having transmuted into one of the most exalted terms in the language. See chapter 9, n. 12 and the biography of Sun Bin in the introduction.

WU. Martial, military (contrasts with *wen*). The character used to write this word shows a shafted weapon and a foot, i.e., a man going off to fight in a war.

XING. Form, shape, disposition. One of the most important tactical concepts in the *Sun Zi*, it occurs with particularly high frequency in chapter 6, where it means mainly the arrangement of forces, and in chapter 10, where it signifies different types of terrain. There is another word, meaning "punishment," that is pronounced exactly alike (*xing*) and is written with a very similar character that one might well expect to find in a work of strategy such as the *Sun Zi*, but it does not occur even once.

The *xing* meaning "form, shape, disposition" occurs a total of thirty-one times in the *Sun Zi*. In stark contrast, the *xing* meaning "punishment" occurs a total of twenty-four times in the *Wei Liao Zi*, a work which has very little to say about the *xing* meaning "form, shape, disposition." Thus the *Sun Zi* and the *Wei Liao Zi*, which probably coalesced at approximately the same time (the second half of the fourth century and the early third century, though with the *Wei Liao Zi* being slightly later) may be said to be in mutual complementarity with regard to the advocacy of these two key concepts of strategy. Clearly the *Sun Zi* is concerned with tactics but not punishment, and vice versa for the *Wei Liao Zi*. Similar analyses could be carried out for other principal concepts in all of the extant military treatises from the Warring States and Han periods.

ZHAN. Battle; specific military actions and engagements, in contrast to *bing* (q.v.), which is more general and abstract.

ZHENG. Used in combination with *qí* to signify contrasting types of warfare; variously translated as "direct/indirect," "regular/irregular," "conventional/unconventional," "orthodox/unorthodox," "ordinary/extraordinary," and so forth. Of these two terms, the more difficult to grasp is *qí*, which may be thought of as signifying "odd, strange, singular, unique, craft(y)" or whatever is not *zheng* ("straight, upright, correct, right, orthodox, normative," etc). In purely military applications, *qí* may be thought of as "special operations" or "unconventional warfare," whereas *zheng* are main force deployments and maneuvers. The counterposing of *qí* and *zheng* was not restricted merely to military operations but was applied to politics and morality as well:

Rule the state with uprightness,
Deploy your troops with craft
Gain all under heaven with noninterference.

(*Tao te Ching/Dao de jing*, 57)

When there is no uprightness,
  correct reverts to crafty,
  good reverts to gruesome.
  (*Tao te Ching/Dao de jing,* 58)

AH	*The American Heritage Dictionary of the English Language,* 4th ed. (Boston: Houghton Mifflin, 2000)
b.	born
c.	century
ca.	circa
chap.	chapter
d.	died
fl.	flourished
HDC	*Hanyu da cidian* (see under Luo Zhufeng in the bibliography)
MSM	Modern Standard Mandarin
n.	note
no.	number
q.v.	*quod vide* (which see)
r.	reigned
RH	*The Random House Dictionary of the English Language,* 2nd ed., unabridged (New York: Random House, 1983)
s.	scroll ([*juan*] of ancient Chinese books)
s.v.	*sub verbo* (under the word [in question])

Sun Zi bingfa (Master Sun's military methods) is the earliest and most important Chinese book that deals exclusively with strategy and tactics. Although it is traditionally attributed to an obscure individual named Sun Wu, who is supposed to have flourished around the end of the sixth century and early fifth century B.C., modern scholarship has demonstrated conclusively that the work evolved during the second half of the fourth century and the beginning of the third century B.C. It is clear, furthermore, that the *Sun Zi* incorporates military lore that circulated broadly during the Warring States period (475–221 B.C.) and could not possibly have been exclusively the product of a single individual.

The *Sun Zi* deals neither with the specifics of training soldiers nor with details concerning the use of various weapons. Rather, it is concerned more with the overall planning for war and especially with the significance of diverse types of terrain. Moreover, espionage is awarded a special place as the concluding chapter of the book. As such, the *Sun Zi* is less concrete than the works of Western military thinkers such as the ancient Greek and Roman strategists or Clausewitz. On the other hand, the generalities of the

Sun Zi have made it highly adaptable for application in business and even for personal decision making.

The present volume emphasizes the unusual style and composition of the *Sun Zi,* its Taoistic aspects, its historical context, its technological presuppositions, and its place in global developments. Those who are interested in these dimensions of the text are invited to read the lengthy introduction and extensive annotations. Those who are interested primarily in the text itself are urged to turn directly to p. 76 and to consult the ancillary materials as they wish.

The Art of War

The Book and Its Title

The Chinese title of the book translated here is *Sun Zi bingfa* or just *Sun Zi*.[1] The latter means simply *Master Sun,* while the former may be rendered as *Master Sun's Military Methods/ Tactics/Strategy*.[2] It is commonly referred to in English as *Master Sun's Art of War* or the *Sun Zi.*

The *Sun Zi* is China's earliest extant work dealing with military affairs.[3] It is held by modern critical scholarship to be the late Warring States (475–221 B.C.) crystallization and summation of the military experiences leading up to that period. It is not, as traditionally believed, the original product of a single author who supposedly lived during the late sixth and early fifth century B.C.

Despite its obscure origins, the *Sun Zi* has had an enormous influence on the development of Chinese military strategy during the last two millennia and occupies an important place in East Asian intellectual history. The *Sun Zi* is concerned with the theory and tactics of war, not such mundane matters as training and practice.

Although it mentions "arrow" once in passing, it does not have anything to say about bows, swords, knives, halberds (*ge*), and spears (*mao*), nor does it utter a word about the drilling of soldiers.

The *Sun Zi bingfa* was by no means the only *bingfa* that appeared during late–Warring States times. We shall encounter the *Wu Zi bingfa* (Master Wu's military methods) and the *Sun Bin bingfa* (Sun Bin's military methods) in our investigations, and there were many others, some associated with a specific individual, and some referred to simply and generically as *bingfa*. In certain cases, we know of a given *bingfa* that initially circulated independently but was later absorbed into a larger text. A good example of the latter situation is *Guan Zi* (Master Guan) VI, 17, a military treatise (c. 250 B.C.) that is even more closely associated with Taoist views than the *Sun Zi bingfa*, which I consider to be "Taoistic" in nature (see below), though the *bingfa* in the *Guan Zi* is also informed with Legalist ideas (Rickett 1985:267–78). What is more, *bingfa* was not the only category of military manuals that circulated during the Warring States period. For instance, in the *Zuo zhuan* (Chronicle of Zuo; completed near the end of the fourth c. B.C.), under the twenty-eighth year (632 B.C.) of Duke Xi, there are three successive quotations from a *Jun zhi* (Treatise on the army): "When things are suitably arranged, then return." "When you realize that you are in difficulty, then retreat." "He who is possessed of *virtūs* cannot be opposed." The fact that the *Zuo zhuan* also quotes from the *Jun zhi* under the twelfth year of Duke Xuan (see *Sun Zi* 7, n. 5) means that this must have been a fairly well established text, since it is quoted in the same authoritative fashion as the *Shi jing* (Classic of poetry) and the *Yi jing* (*Classic of Change*). And *Sun Zi* 7 itself quotes from an obviously earlier text called the *Jun zheng* (Army administration) about the need for efficient signaling in the heat of battle.

Elements of the military thought of the *Sun Zi* are to be found in other noted late–Warring States works dealing with strategy,

such as the *Wu Zi, Sun Bin bingfa*, and *Wei Liao Zi* (alternate pronunciation: *Yu Liao Zi*; Master Wei Liao [or Yu Liao]).[4] In any
event, there is no doubt that the reputation of the *Sun Zi* was
firmly established by the beginning of the first century B.C.[5]

It seems ironic that, of all the military treatises that appeared
during the latter part of the Warring States and Han periods,[6] the
Sun Zi is the least likely to be connected to an actual person. On
the other hand, it may simply be the case that, once the *Sun Zi*
congealed into stable written form, it provided a model for the
composition of other military texts that were more closely linked
to known individuals.

An important aspect of the history of the *Sun Zi* is the commentarial tradition that grew up around it and sustained it during the first and second millennia A.D. Over the centuries, there
have been at least two hundred different commentaries written
on the *Sun Zi*. Few of those composed after the Han period have
any significant philological or historical value, though they are
of interest for understanding the ongoing importance of the *Sun
Zi* during medieval and later imperial history. Of these, there are
about a dozen that stand out and are most frequently cited. Con-
veniently, these have been brought together in *Shiyi jia zhu Sun
Zi* (The *Sun Zi* with annotations by eleven commentators) compiled by Ji Tianbao (eleventh to twelfth c.). The eleven commentators[7] are Cao Cao (155–220), Meng shi (Mr. Meng, Liang Dynasty
[502–557]), Li Quan (fl. 750), Jia Lin (around the last quarter of
the eighth c.), Du You (735–812),[8] Du Mu (803–852), Chen Hao
(late Tang), Mei Yaochen (1002–1060), Wang Xi (fl. 1082), He
Yanxi (after the mid-eleventh c.), and Zhang Yu (Southern Song
[1127–1279]). All of these individuals clearly had a strong interest
in military matters, but we know almost nothing else concerning
over half of them.

Cao Cao was a famous military leader during the latter part of
the Eastern Han (25–220) who was responsible for the initiation

of the Three Kingdoms period (220–280 A.D.). It was Cao Cao who wrote the first (and by far the most valuable) commentary on the *Sun Zi*, and I shall have occasion to cite it more than any other in my own notes. In his preface to the *Sun Zi* preserved in his collected writings, Cao Cao praised it lavishly: "I have read many soldierly books and military stratagems. The one written by Sun Wu is the most profound." The great Tang (618–907) emperor, Taizong (Li Shimin 599–649, r. 627–649), when discussing soldierly methods with his outstanding general, Li Jing (571–649), extolled the *Sun Zi* in similar terms: "Of the soldierly books that I have read, none is superior to the *Sun Zi*."

Although little information is available about Li Quan, he is noteworthy because he was a Taoist and because he had an interest in martial arts. After a moderately successful official career, reaching to the level of provincial governor, he was demoted and thereafter became a wandering Taoist recluse. The place of his reclusion was the same mountain (Song Shan), north of present-day Dengfeng County, Henan Province, that earlier was supposed to have been the abode of Bodhidharma, the first Zen (Chan) patriarch in East Asia. It is here too that Shaolin Monastery, with its celebrated tradition of fighting monks, is located (Rand 1979; Shahar 2001).

Du You was a highly distinguished scholar and statesman, thrice a chancellor at the Tang court. He is best known, however, for his compilation of the encyclopedic *Tongdian* (Comprehensive institutions; completed in 801), a rich collection of information pertaining to political and administrative affairs. One of the nine main sections of the *Tongdian* is devoted to border defenses and includes a wealth of authoritative material concerning Central Asian military matters. This is in large measure due to his nephew Du Huan's having been taken captive at the Battle of the Talas River in July 751 at the town of Atlakh (near Talas) in what is now northwestern Kirghizstan. Located approximately two-thirds of the way from Frunze (capital of Kirghizstan, formerly known as Pishpek or Bishbek) to Dzambul (in Kazakhstan), this is the site of one of the most important battles in the history of the world. Here an Arab army of the Abbasid Caliphate defeated a Chinese army under the Korean general Go Seonji (or Ko Sôn-ji; MSM Gao Xianzhi; d. 756), thereby halting the expansion of the Tang toward the west and establishing the foundations for the dominance of Islam in Central Asia for the coming centuries. An incidental, but far from inconsequential repercussion of the battle of Talas River is that, among the Chinese captives, aside from Du Huan, there were also paper makers who subsequently transmitted their craft to West Asia. Du Huan's lost memoir, *Jingxing ji* (Notes on places passed through) was incorporated into Du You's *Tongdian*. After visiting Arabia, Du Huan returned by sea in 762, having been away for a total of nearly a dozen years. An interesting tie-in with Li Quan is that Du You also draws on a military treatise completed by him in 768 and Taoistically entitled *Taibo yin jing* (Scripture of Venusian *yin*) (Wakeman 1990:6–7). Despite the mystical title, the *Taibo yin jing* is actually tough-minded and pragmatic, declaring that success in war is dependent upon human abilities and intelligence, not yin and yang.

Another member of the distinguished Du family who was so absorbed in military matters that he wrote a commentary on the *Sun Zi* is Du Mu, one of the finest late Tang poets. But Du Mu was not the only outstanding poet to write a commentary on the *Sun Zi*, for he was followed in that calling by Mei Yaochen, one of the best known early Song poets.

It is evident that the *Sun Zi*, though slight of scope and of obscure origins, has attracted some of the best minds—military, scholarly, religious, poetic, and even royal—throughout history until the present day.[9] Wherein lies the mystique of this diminutive text? For one thing, the *Sun Zi* is to war as the *Tao te ching/Dao de jing* is to mysticism—in more ways than one, as we shall see momentarily. But the sheer prismatic nature of the *Sun Zi* accounts for a large measure of its popularity, since the text is viewed in a variety of lights depending upon which facet one focuses upon.

The first woodblock printed editions of the *Sun Zi* date to the Song period (960–1279).[10] The earliest extant is preserved in the *Wu jing qi shu* (Seven military classics) from sometime during the reign of Emperor Ningzong (r. 1195–1224).[11] Together with the *Shiyi jia zhu Sun Zi* mentioned above, this is the edition that I shall refer to as the "received text."[12] It is contrasted with archeologically recovered manuscript finds, which take us back much nearer to the time when the text was composed.

In 1972, at Yinque Shan (Silver Sparrow Mountain) in Linyi County (about 120 miles southwest of Qingdao), Shandong Province, a small cluster of closely related Western Han tombs dating to between about 140 and 118 B.C. was discovered. From these tombs were unearthed more than five thousand bamboo strips, including a large quantity of fragmentary texts dealing with military matters. Among them was the earliest known copy of the *Sun Zi*. In addition to the thirteen chapters of the received text (so far only the title of the tenth chapter has been identified among the manuscript finds), five other fragmentary texts closely associated with the *Sun Zi* were recovered from the same tombs.[13]

Even more significant, the hitherto lost work known as *Sun Bin bingfa* (hereafter *Sun Bin* for short) was also found among the Yinque Shan manuscripts.[14] As we shall see below in the next section discussing authorship, the chances that there existed an actual historical personage called Sun Bin (ca. 380–320 B.C.) are far greater than that there was a real individual behind the "Master Sun" of the *Sun Zi*. Sun Bin's major defeat of the forces of the state of Wei under Pang Juan in a famous battle of 341 B.C. at Maling[15] is mentioned at least three different times in the *Shi ji* (*The Grand Scribe's Records*, s. 65, 68, and 75),[16] and each time it is convincingly linked with historically verifiable persons or dates (Nienhauser 1994:xviii, 41, 91, 190). The intricate interdependence between the *Sun Zi* and the *Sun Bin*, together with the other fragmentary texts associated with them, is a topic that I shall touch upon at various points in this investigation. Since all of these texts were recovered from the Western Han tombs at Yinque Shan and were written on bamboo strips, I shall henceforth refer to them as the Yinque Shan (bamboo strip) manuscripts.

The Yinque Shan site may lie within the southern reaches of Qi, the northern state that Sun Bin served, and it is close to the territory of the much smaller state of Lu, from which Confucius (ca. 550–479 B.C.) hailed.[17] Although the tombs contained a considerable quantity of military works, no weapons have been found, giving the impression that this was a family deeply interested (and probably highly expert) in military matters, but not professional soldiers.

The bamboo strips from Yinque Shan are not the only early manuscripts related to the *Sun Zi* that have recently been archeologically recovered. A late Western Han tomb (first century B.C.) at Shang Sunjia Zhai (Upper Sun Family Fortress) in Datong County, Qinghai Province[18] (in the remote northwestern part of China) has also yielded important military documents. Although the expression *Sun Zi yue* ("Master Sun said") occurs five times in these documents, they do not constitute an early edition of the *Sun Zi*. Rather, they are a collection of old military orders, some of which invoke the storied "Master Sun" to enhance their authority. None of the quotations attributed to "Master Sun" in the Shang Sunjia Zhai manuscripts can be found in the received text or among the supplemental passages in later literature that are associated with it (Li 1995:261). Another noteworthy aspect of the Shang Sunjia Zhai manuscripts is that they three times mention cavalry, a subject that is entirely absent from the *Sun Zi*. All of this indicates that, in addition to the *Sun Zi* and the *Sun Bin*, there must have been a large body of military lore attributed to "Master Sun" that circulated broadly during the Western Han and probably already during the late–Warring States period as well. It was from this amorphous corpus of "Master Sun" materials that the various editions of the *Sun Zi* and the *Sun Bin* recorded in early bibliographies must have been compiled. The fact that the available body of materials was much bigger than any of the individual collections would account for the discrepancies in length and contents among the various editions of the *Sun Zi*. Indeed, this same indeterminate reservoir of military wisdom would also have been drawn upon by the other strategists who emerged during the late–Warring States and Han periods. Nonetheless, it is essential to observe that one of the fragmentary Shang Sunjia Zhai wooden strips (no. 061) reads as follows: "Master Sun said, 'Now, the thirteen chapters. . .'." Here "Master Sun" is referring to the work that has been linked with the illusory Sun Wu since at least the Western Han period.

Like the even more influential ancient Chinese classic, the *Tao te ching* (*Dao de jing*), which has a total of only about five thousand characters, the *Sun Zi* is a short work, with a total of some six thousand characters. Yet it manages to cover a variety of vital topics in its thirteen chapters. In terms of general principles, the *Sun Zi* identifies and advocates the following: awareness of the political and psychological aspects of war, the importance of careful calculation and planning before embarking on a campaign, mastery of different types of terrain and the appropriate disposition of forces in relation to them, and the ability to capitalize upon favorable circumstances and to avoid unfavorable circumstances. Two chapters on incendiary warfare and espionage are not integral to the main concerns of the *Sun Zi* but are late additions, probably by persons holding a brief for these specialized aspects of warfare. Since the text has nothing to say about chariots, cavalry, and bowmen, it is obvious that the *Sun Zi* was assembled with mass infantry in mind.

AUTHORSHIP

Every chapter of the *Sun Zi* begins with the incipit, "Master Sun said." This mechanical invocation of "Master Sun" implies nothing more or less than a vague persona who supposedly uttered all of the wise sayings in the book that goes by his name. Here in the introduction and in the annotations, when reference is made to "Master Sun," it signifies the collective personality of all military sages whose pronouncements were assembled in the *Sun Zi*. By no means should use of the name "Sun Zi" or "Master Sun" in the introduction and commentary be construed as indicating acceptance of a particular individual as the author of the entire text. In short, the author of the *Sun Zi* is a fictional entity, and any mention of him in this volume should be thought of as having quotation marks around it, indicating that he is "the so-called Master Sun" or "the so-called Sun Wu."

The Danish Sinologist Jens Østergård Petersen has persuasively demonstrated (1992a) that the stories told about Sun Wu are generic in nature. They are illustrative tales that are repeated (often with only minor variations) about different individuals, some real, some not. Petersen has also subjected to intense scrutiny the various names applied to Master Sun (Sun Zi, Sun Wǔ, Sun Wú, and Wǔ Zi)[19] and has determined (1992b) that they are all problematic as references to a specific person who is alleged to have been active in the latter part of the Spring and Autumn period (770–476 B.C.). Indeed, two of the names—Sun Wú and Sun Zi—more often than not refer to Sun Bin, who lived in the Warring States period, while Wǔ Zi is an implausible title, and Sun Wǔ itself lacks historical grounding. It is also noteworthy that the names Sun Wǔ and Sun Bin do not occur among the Yinque Shan manuscripts, only Sun Zi, which could refer to either or both.[20] Furthermore, the first occurrence of the name Sun Wǔ is in the *Shi ji*, which was completed shortly after 87 B.C. Thus, "Sun Zi" in Han

and earlier texts—if it signifies any specific person—generally refers to Sun Bin, who was a known entity in pre-Han times, whereas
Sun Wŭ was not (Petersen 1992b).

Sun Wŭ's name itself has all the marks of being a made-up cognomen that is descriptive of his role in the extensively studied Wu
Zixu story (Rudolph 1942, 1962; Johnson 1980, 1981; Mair 1983).[21]
That is to say, like the hero Wu Zixu of the Spring and Autumn
period, he *flees* to Wú, and like Wu Zixu, he is a *warrior,* where
Sun (literally "grandson") signifies *xun* ("flee, abdicate")[22] and Wŭ
directly means "military, martial, valiant," hence Sun (i.e., Xun)
Wŭ may be translated as "the fugitive warrior." The difference,
however, is that Wu Zixu had a reason for fleeing from Chu (the
murder of his father and brother by the king), whereas Sun Wu's
reason for fleeing from Qi (his alleged home state) is completely
unknown.[23] Overall, the function of the Sun Wŭ persona in the
initial stage of its development as part of the Wu Zixu story is to
serve as a reinforcing *Doppelgänger* for the central hero. The inspiration for the creation of the Sun Wu character may have come
from Sun Bin, who was actually a military specialist from Qi, but
who flourished approximately a century and a half after the time
that Sun Wŭ was alleged to have lived. Once launched as a supporting member of the cast of the Wu Zixu drama, the Sun Wŭ
character was free to develop as an independent figure in military
lore.

There is a great deal of evidence that Sun Bin was a genuine
authority on military affairs, but that—through a curious process akin to euhemerization—a legendary figure called Sun Wu
emerged as the Sun Zi ("Master Sun") who was acknowledged as
the fountain of military wisdom, and not Sun Bin. Some of the
evidence for the spinning off of Sun Wu from Sun Bin is presented
elsewhere in the introduction and in the notes to this volume.
Here, however, I examine one particularly telling item. Namely, in
Lü shi chunqiu (Spring and Autumn annals of Mr. Lü; an eclectic

text of about 240 B.C.) 17.7, it states explicitly that "Sun Bin valued *shi* ('configuration')." It is obvious that *shi* is also extremely important for the *Sun Zi*, since it occurs a total of fifteen times in the text, eight times in chapter 5 (one of the shortest chapters in the book) alone. *Shi* occurs only a total of three times in the other three major works on military strategy from Han and earlier times that were part of the received tradition (*Wei Liao Zi, Wu Zi*, and *Sima fa*), thus there are five times as many instances of *shi* in the *Sun Zi* as in the other three main military treatises put together. *Shi* also occurs often in the *Sun Bin*, and chapter 9, entitled "Shi bei" (Preparation of configuration), is devoted to it. Hence, it would appear that Sun Bin was a specialist in *shi* and was recognized for his expertise in this crucial aspect of tactics. However, in the formation of the *Sun Zi*, some of that expertise was siphoned off, with the result that the fictitious Sun Wu also became an expert on *shi*.

The proliferation of Sun Zi lore did not stop with the establishment of the thirteen-chapter edition as the *Sun Zi*. Sun Zi dialogs and Sun Zi narratives continued to coalesce in an amorphous repository. This accounts for the *Sun Zi* editions with nearly a hundred chapters (counting scrolls of illustrations) listed in Han-period and other bibliographies, and it also explains the unruly collection of Sun Zi texts among the Yinque Shan and Shang Sun-jia Zhai manuscripts that are, more often than not, impossible to assign with confidence either to the *Sun Zi* or to the *Sun Bin*.[24]

Nor did the flourishing industry of writing tactics and strategies stop with Sun Wu and Sun Bin. It was inevitable that texts would come to be associated with other military authorities as well, whether they were real, imagined, or somewhere in between. Once the writing of military treatises was legitimized by the creation of the *Sun Zi*, it spawned a bevy of competing texts. After the Sun dyad (Sun Bin and his more famous alter ego, Sun Wu), probably the first out of the chute was Wú Qi, whose *Wú Zi* swiftly came to be paired with the *Sun Zi* as the dual fount of military *sagesse* (hence the expression Sun Wú). After that came the *Wei Liao Zi* and the *Sima fa,* with the authors of the *Sun Zi* and the *Sima fa* tending more to the side of legend and the authors of the *Sun Bin* and the *Wú Zi* being somewhat more securely grounded in history.

To summarize the sequence of Warring States military treatises as they appeared beginning from the middle of the fourth c. B.C., the first to be compiled was the *Sun Zi.* The *Sun Bin* most likely did not coagulate until the early Han period, after the *Sun Zi* was securely established, and was loosely formed from the residue of Sun Zi materials left over after the compilation of the *Sun Zi.* The *Wu Zi* probably would have come in between, and it has more earmarks of a composed text than the compilatory *Sun Zi* and *Sun Bin* (the latter less so than the former).

Although careful textual and historical research indicates that we should be wary of assigning the composition of the *Sun Zi* to a single individual, the book itself clearly adopts the pretense of embodying the *ipsissima verba* of a certain Master Sun. This formula ("Master Sun said") by itself, however, gives probable evidence that the text was compiled by another or others who came after the putative military pundit.

The conventional view, nonetheless, is that the author was a man named Sun Wu who was a great military theorist and who allegedly lived around the end of the Spring and Autumn period, making him a contemporary of Confucius. He is said to have been a man of the state of Qi (in the northeast) who—for some unknown reason—fled to the southeastern kingdom of Wu. There he was introduced by the high official Wu Zixu (also called Wu Yuan or Wu Yu; late sixth–early fifth c. B.C.), himself a refugee from the south-central state of Chu, to the king of Wu, Helu (or Helü) (r. 514–496 B.C.). A fanciful tale of Sun Wu training the palace ladies of King Helu constitutes almost the whole of his sole "biography" (see appendix). Impressed by Sun Wu's ability to train even beautiful women to obey military commands implicitly and to face death and danger unflinchingly, the king appoints him as a general in the Wu army. Together with Wu Zixu, Sun Wu helps the king of Wu administer the state and train the army. As a result, the kingdom of Wu grows to be so powerful that it is able to defeat its enemy to the west, the great state of Chu, entering the Chu capital of Ying,[25] and further to intimidate the strong states of Qi and Jin to the north.

Given such a skimpy "life," it is not surprising that Sun Wu enthusiasts of later times concocted a few more biographical details. More than a millennium and a half after the time when he was supposed to have lived, Sun Wu is first identified as having been from a place called Le'an (it is disputed whether that corresponds to modern Boxing [pronounced Buosheeng] County or Huimin County in Shandong Province);[26] his grandfather is said to have been granted a fief there. This is casually mentioned, without any proof or documentation, in the "Zaixiang shixi biao" (Genealogical chart of the grand councilors) of the *Xin Tang shu* (New history of the Tang Dynasty [73B: 2945]), which was completed in 1060 A.D.

Starting with the Song Dynasty scholar Ye Shi (1150–1223), doubts have sensibly been raised over the historicity of Sun Wu.[27] It has been suggested by some scholars that Sun Wu and Sun Bin (who is supposed by Sima Qian to be a descendant of Sun Wu and whose biography follows immediately after his in the *Shi ji*) may have been the same person. This is virtually impossible, however, since Sun Bin lived more than a century after Sun Wu, as asserted at the very beginning of his biography in the *Shi ji*. Sun Bin's placement in the second half of the fourth century, roughly a hundred and fifty years after the purported time of Sun Wu, is corroborated by the kings (Hui [r. 369–335 B.C.] of Wei and Wei [r. 356–320 B.C.] of Qi) and the generals (Pang Juan [fl. mid-fourth c. B.C.] and Tian Ji [fl. second half of the fourth c. B.C.]) with whom he was associated. It is far more likely that Sun Bin was a historical figure (ca. 380–ca. 325 B.C.) and that Sun Wu is a figmentary extrapolation from him.[28]

Suspicion of Sun Wu's historicity goes hand in hand with doubt over his authorship of the *Sun Zi* and its dating to the Spring and Autumn period. Henri Maspero said of the *Sun Zi*, "The work, if not a complete forgery, must date, at the earliest, from the third century B.C.; and it can therefore have nothing to do either with Sun Pin [i.e., Bin] or with his fabulous ancestor [Sun Wu]" (1978:441n. 3; 1955: 328n. 1). Written long before the discovery of the Yinque Shan and Shang Sunjia Zhai manuscripts, this is an amazingly prescient, perceptive remark.

The given names of both Sun Wu and Sun Bin are peculiar. The former means "Martial," and the latter means "Kneecapped."[29] Thus, their full names would mean "Sun the Martial" and "Sun the Kneecapped," or, in Western order, "Martial Sun" and "Kneecapped Sun." Whereas the first is simply too pat, too neat for the presumed father of all military theory in China, the latter is most certainly not a sufficiently grand name for a nation's foremost military authority. Since, as I have shown in various ways, the real "Sun Zi" was Sun Bin, it is easy to understand the psychological motivation, indeed necessity, to transform "Kneecapped Sun" into "Martial Sun."

The story of how Sun Bin got his bizarre name is worth retelling in this context, since it has deep implications, both for the development of the Sun Zi legends and for their codification in China's first standard history, the *Shi ji* (*The Grand Scribe's Records*). Since it is not overly long and is full of vital information concerning the establishment of the Sun Zi legends for the rest of Chinese history, it is worth citing the entire biography of Sun Bin from the *Shi ji*:

> More than a hundred years after Sun Wu died there was Sun Bin. Bin was born between E and Juan.[30] He was a descendant

of Sun Wu. Sun Bin once studied the methods of war [*bingfa*] together with Pang Juan. After Pang Juan took up service in Wei, he obtained a command under King Hui [r. 370–335 B.C.], but thought his own ability inferior to Sun Bin's and secretly had a man summon Sun Bin. When Bin arrived, Pang Juan grew fearful that he was more worthy than himself. Jealous of Sun Bin, Pang Juan had both his feet cut off and his face tattooed as punishment by law,[31] hoping that Sun would retire and refuse to appear.

An envoy from Qi went to Liang.[32] Sun Bin, since he was a convict who had suffered the punishment of mutilation, met with the Qi envoy in secret and advised him. The Qi envoy thought him remarkable and secretly carried Bin to Qi with him in his carriage. Qi's general Tian Ji thought much of Sun Bin and made him his guest. Ji raced horses and gambled heavily with the Noble Scions of Qi several times. Sun Zi noticed that the horses' speed was not much different and that the horses fell into high, middle, and low grades. After this, Sun Zi told Tian Ji, "Just bet heavily, My Lord, and I can make you the winner."

Tian Ji confidently agreed and bet a thousand pieces of gold with King Wei [r. 378–343 B.C.] and the Noble Scions of Qi on a race. Just before the wager Sun Zi said, "Now match their high-grade horses with your low-grade horses, take your high-grade horses to match their middle-grade horses, and take your middle-grade horses to match their low-grade horses."

After they raced the three grades of horses, Tian Ji lost once but won twice and eventually gained the king's thousand pieces of gold. After this, Ji presented Sun Zi to King Wei. King Wei questioned him on the arts of war and made him his counselor.

Some time later, Wei attacked Zhao. Zhao was hard pressed and sought help from Qi. King Wei of Qi wanted to make Sun

Bin commander, but Sun declined: "A mutilated criminal will never do." King Wei then made Tian Ji commander and Sun Zi his counselor.

Sun occupied a wagon where he sat and drew up plans and strategies [*ji mou*].[33] Tian Ji wanted to lead the troops to Zhao. Sun Zi said, "To untangle a snarled mess, one does not raise his fists, and to stop a fight one does not grab or bind. Seize him at his throat and charge him where he is defenseless; his formations attacked, his power constrained, he will retire of his own accord.[34] Liang and Zhao are attacking each other now; their swift soldiers and picked troops are sure to be exhausted outside on the battlefield, their aged and infirm exhausted inside the cities. It would be better for My Lord to lead the troops in a rush to Da Liang; block its roads and highways, and strike it when still undefended. Liang is sure to release Zhao and save itself. We would thus in one swoop raise the siege of Zhao and exhaust Wei [i.e., Liang]."

Tian Ji followed his advice, and Wei did indeed leave Handan[35] and fought with Qi at Guiling.[36] Qi crushed the Liang army.

Thirteen years later, Wei and Zhao attacked Han. Han informed Qi of its straits. Qi had Tian Ji take command and go to Han's rescue. He rushed straight to Da Liang. Wei's commander Pang Juan[37] heard this, left Han, and returned to Wei, but Qi's army had already passed him and advanced west into Wei.

Sun Zi told Tian Ji, "These troops of Three Jin[38] have always been both fierce and courageous, and have little regard for Qi, since Qi has a name for cowardice. A skilled fighter acts according to the situation and directs the course of events by offering the enemy advantages. According to the arts of war, "'when one races after advantage for a hundred tricents, the commander falls; when one races after advantage for fifty tricents, only half the army arrives.'" When Qi's army enters Wei territory, have them make cooking fires for a hundred thousand; the next day make fires for fifty thousand; and the day after make fires for thirty thousand."

On the third day of Pang Juan's march, Pang rejoiced. "I knew Qi's troops were cowards; three days after entering our territory, over half their officers and men have fled." He abandoned his infantry and covered two days' distance in one day with lightly armed, picked soldiers, pursuing Qi's troops. Sun Zi judged that they would reach Maling[39] at dusk. The road through Maling was narrow and there were numerous barriers on both sides where troops could be hidden. Sun stripped the bark off a great tree and carved on it, "Pang Juan died at the foot of this tree." After this he ordered the best archers in Qi's army to hide along both sides of the road with ten thousand crossbows[40] and arranged a signal. "When you see a brand at dusk, fire in concert."

As he expected, Pang Juan reached the foot of the stripped tree at night, saw the inscription, and struck a fire to illuminate it. Before he had finished reading Sun's inscription, the Qi army's ten thousand crossbows all fired at once, and Wei's army was thrown into chaos and confusion. Pang Juan, realizing that he had been outwitted and his troops defeated, cut his throat: "Now this whelp's name is made!"

The Qi army, following up on their victory, crushed Pang's army, captured Wei's heir, Shen, and returned. Sun Bin's name was renowned throughout the world because of this; his *bingfa* ["methods of war"] is transmitted to the present generation.[41]

In terms of its specificity and historical groundedness, this is a far more believable biography than the account of Sun Wu which directly precedes it in *Shi ji* 65. It should be noted that "Sun Zi" (Master Sun) in this biography clearly refers to Sun Bin, not Sun Wu.[42]

Sima Qian, author of the *Shi ji,* must have felt a poignant affinity with Sun Bin, for he had suffered the ultimate mutilation and humiliation of castration (Goldin 2005b). Furthermore, this was the result of his speaking out in defense of a general who had been defeated by the northern nomads (Xiongnu/Huns) and defected to them. Sima sublimated his grief by pouring all his remaining energy into writing the *Shi ji,* which survives to this day as a monument to China's first historian. Ban Gu (32–92 A.D.), author of the *Han shu* (History of the Han; the second of China's twenty-four standard histories) and member of a distinguished family that had both military and Xiongnu (Hunnish, north[west]ern) connections, wrote a sympathetic biography of Sima Qian. In it, he draws the obvious parallel that "Sun Zi suffered the mutilation of having his feet amputated, [in consequence of which] he composed his *bingfa* ['methods of war']" (*Han shu* 62: 2735; my translation). Since the mutilation is specified by the term *bin,* there can be no doubt whatsoever that Ban Gu is referring to Sun Bin and not to Sun Wu when he mentions Sun Zi.

There is an overlap of materials between the *Sun Zi* and the *Sun Bin* (Goldin 2005a). *Sun Bin* is a later development presupposing the previous existence of the *Sun Zi,* "and the two may well form a single, continuously developing intellectual tradition united under the Sun name" (Lewis 2005:6).

As much as anyone, Sima Qian, author of the *Shi ji,* was responsible for promoting the Sun Zi (= Sun Wu) cult,[43] yet even he—at a crucial moment—let slip that he must have been aware of the fact that the real Sun Zi was Sun Bin and not the imaginary Sun Wu. This occurs in his closing comments to the combined biographies of Sun Wǔ, Sun Bin, and Wú Qi (*Shi ji,* s. 65):

> When the world talks about armies and brigades, they all mention the thirteen chapters of the *Sun Zi* and Wu Qi's *Military Methods.* Most people in the world have these books, therefore

I have not discussed them here, but instead have discussed the implementation of their actions. A common saying has it that "Those who can act cannot necessarily speak, and those who can speak cannot necessarily act." Master Sun was brilliant in his calculations against Pang Juan, but could not save himself earlier from the disaster of mutilation. Wu Qi advised Marquis Wu that form and configuration[44] were not as important as *virtūs*,[45] but when he applied this principle in Chu, he destroyed himself through his harsh tyranny and lack of mercy. How sad![46]

Whether "Sun Zi" in late–Warring States times referred to the imaginary Sun Wŭ or the real Sun Bin,[47] there is no doubt that he (Sun Zi) and his book of strategy had become indelibly linked to Wú Qi and his manual of tactics by that time.[48] From around the mid-third c. B.C., "Sun Wú" (meaning "Sun Zi" and "Wú Qi," together with their works) functioned as a nearly ubiquitous expression for military savoir faire.

The *Lü shi chunqiu* (Spring and Autumn annals of Mr. Lü) has a postface dated 239 B.C. It is suggestive that when (in 19.3) it mentions Sun and Wú we might be witnessing the legend of Sun Wŭ at an incipient stage of development, when it is still rather inchoate. In this passage, we cannot be sure which Sun (Zi) is being referred to, although Wú most likely specifies Wú Qi. Together, they are loosely linked with King Helu of Wú, which is fine for the emerging Sun Zi (Sun Wŭ), but not for Wú Qi. According to his biography in *Shi ji* 65, Wú Qi was a northerner from the state of Wey who spent the first part of his life in service to monarchs of the northern states of Wei and Lu, and the latter part in the southern state of Chu. There is no indication of his having anything to do with Helu of the southeastern state of Wú. Still, having this vague mid-third-century B.C. reference to a Sun (Zi) and another eminent military expert mentioned in the same breath with King

Helu of Wú might well explain how, by the beginning of the second century B.C., we have an elaborate legend involving Sun Wǔ and Wu Zixu assisting the king of Wu in successfully defeating its archenemy, Chu.

The paradigmatic pair of Sun (Zi) and Wú (Qi) occurs three times in the Legalistic text ascribed to Han Fei Zi (Master Han Fei [ca. 280–233 B.C.]). A careful analysis of these occurrences offers revealing evidence for the conundrum of how Sun Bin begat his own ancestor. *Han Fei Zi* 26 is entitled "Shou dao" (Guarding the way). Near the end of this chapter, the author declares that, in a Legalist utopia, "The strategies of Sun [and] Wú would be abandoned, the intentions of Robber Footpad would be cowed." Robber Footpad (Dao Zhe) was an archetypal brigand featured in *Zhuang Zi* 29 (Mair 1994:298–311). Since "Sun Wú" is parallel to "Dao Zhe" here in *Han Fei Zi* 26, it would appear that Sun and Wú have been conflated into a single entity, and conflation may well have been the prelude to fusion. *Han Fei Zi* 49 is entitled "Wu du" (Five vermin). Here the author states that, where Legalist ideals do not yet hold sway, "Within the realm, everyone speaks of war; in each family there are those who preserve copies of the books of Sun [and] Wú."[49] He goes on to decry the fact that, whereas everybody is enamored of military theory, the soldiers are weak and that, while everyone is discussing war, there are few who strap on armor. Here again, this could be a reference to Sun Zi (perhaps an emergent Sun Wǔ) and Wú Qi, but—in the mind of the author—it might also vaguely signify a blurred composite.

The most telling instance of all, however, occurs in *Han Fei Zi* 3, "Nan yan" (Speaking with difficulty): "Master Sun had his kneecaps chopped off in Wei, Wú Qi daubed tears at Cliffgate." Of the fifty-five chapters of the *Han Fei Zi*, chapter 3 is arguably the earliest, the core of the entire text, and probably the only one that dates to the time of the thinker after whom the whole collection is named (Brooks 1994:17–19). It is essential to note that, in this relatively early occurrence of the Sun-Wú dyad, there is no question but that we are dealing with two individuals (not a fuzzy fusion) and there can be no mistaking the fact that these two military experts are none other than Sun Bin and Wú Qi. All the later evocations of "Sun [and] Wú" where "Sun" comes to mean the imagined "Sun Zi" of the Spring and Autumn period, i.e., Sun Wǔ, hearken back to this foundational stage where "Sun" still meant "Sun Bin," *not* "Sun Wǔ." Thus, within the evolving *Han Fei Zi,* we witness the evolving Sun Zi, who develops from Sun Bin to Sun Wǔ. We may compare this transformation to the exuviation of a cicada. When Sun Wǔ emerged from the old Sun Bin shell, he was shiny and splendid, and the old, discarded husk would have been left by the wayside—were it not for the chance archeological discovery of the Yinque Shan bamboo strips, which have restored Sun Bin to his rightful eminence.

The *Xun Zi,* attributed to Xun Qing (fl. mid-third c. B.C.), also has a long chapter on military matters that is entitled "Yi bing" (A discussion of war). It was almost certainly not written by Master Xun himself but composed by one or more of his disciples.[50] Also, the form of the surname used for Xun Zi in this chapter (Sun instead of Xun)[51] indicates that it was written during the Han period (to avoid a taboo on use of the phonophore [phonetic component] of the personal name of the Han emperor Xuan Di, viz., Liu Xun [91–49 B.C.; r. 73–49 B.C.]). It is probably not accidental that the semi-homophonous graph chosen to replace the Xun surname was none other than Sun, which bids fair to capitalize on the glamour of this eponym of strategists. Linwu Jun ("Lord Overseer of the Military"; third c. B.C.[?]), about whom nothing substantial is known, functions as an interlocutor in this chapter. The debate begins with Linwu Jun emphasizing the practical, technical aspects of warfare. He stresses the need to capitalize upon strategic advantage, close observation, and swift action. Xun Zi (in this instance called Sun Qingzi) firmly counters that what really matters is to gain the support of the people, which is one of the tenets proposed near the beginning of *Sun Zi* 1. Linwu Jun responds with another aphoristic assertion from the middle of *Sun Zi* 1, namely, that the most crucial aspects of warfare are transformation and deception. "Those who are skilled at waging war [*shan yong bing zhe*]," he opines, are elusive and mysterious in their comings and goings. He then goes on to state that "Sun and Wú used [these principles], and there was no one under heaven who was a match[52] for them." Now, as in the *Lü shi chunqiu* passage discussed above, we do not know for certain which "Sun" is being referred to here, but given the fact that he is paired with Wú [Qi] and the relatively late date of composition of this part of the *Xun Zi* (late third or early second c. B.C.), most likely it is Sun Wǔ, not Sun Bin, who was already beginning to be eclipsed by his fictive ancestor.

Although the "Master Sun" of the *Sun Zi* (i.e., Sun Wǔ) is a purely legendary figure concerning whom not a shred of reliable biographical data exists, for those who believe in him, he is as real as any deity or mythical hero. It has been so since the second century B.C.

It would appear that the process whereby texts on tactics and strategy came to be written down and assigned to various authors during the Warring States period first emerged around the middle of the fourth century B.C. with the blossoming of the Iron Revolution in East Asia.[53] These beginnings then grew into an embryo, and the embryo soon developed into a full-blown but ill-defined text. Once the thirteen chapters of the *Sun Zi* assumed canonical form (before the middle of the third century B.C.), the residue of Sun Zi materials were shunted off into the *Sun Bin*. This is ironic, since it was Sun Bin who was the initial Sun Zi and around whom the Sun Zi lore began to crystallize into a written corpus.[54] But it is also understandable that Sun Bin would be displaced by Sun Wǔ as *the* Sun Zi (Master Sun), because Sun Wǔ was a purely imaginary figure. Unconstrained by reality, Sun Wǔ evolved as an iconic founding father of East Asian military wisdom. Thus Sun/Xun Wŭ ("the fugitive warrior") was doubly a *Doppelgänger*, first of Wu Zixu (who truly was a fugitive warrior), and second of Sun Bin ("the mutilated grandson").

The firm establishment of the *Sun Zi* as a written text opened the way for the flourishing of additional books of strategy and tactics attributed to other military men, such as the *Wú Zi*, the *Wei Liao Zi*, the *Sima fa*, and so forth. The historicity of the authors to whom these works were ascribed was not essential. What mattered was their charisma and their reputation.

HISTORICAL BACKGROUND

The *Sun Zi* was compiled during the second half of the Warring States period (ca. 475–221 B.C.). Moving backward in time, the Warring States period was preceded by the Spring and Autumn period, which began around 770 B.C. with the weakening of the Zhou king to the point that nearly a dozen major states and many lesser statelets no longer felt themselves beholden to him. The Warring States period saw an intensification of interstate rivalry and a growing tendency to use military force to achieve domination, rather than relying on diplomacy and relatively small-scale armed conflicts to maintain the alliances and balances that had characterized the Spring and Autumn period.

The Zhou Dynasty had begun ca. 1045 B.C. with the defeat of the Shang, the first historically verifiable dynasty in East Asia. The Shang and the Zhou (up through the Spring and Autumn period) belong to the Bronze Age, which was characterized by bronze weapons and chariot warfare (Shaughnessy 1988, 1989), both of which were monopolized by the elites. The Warring States period, which was distinguished by massive infantry armies and iron weaponry (particularly during the latter part), culminated in the unification of the empire under the Qin, a short-lived (221–206

B.C.) but extremely important dynasty that brought an end to the incessant wars of the preceding three centuries.

There is actually no unanimity as to precisely when the Warring States period began. Some say that it started in 481 B.C., when the chronicles of Lu (Confucius' home state) conclude, marking the end of the Spring and Autumn period. Others maintain that the Warring States period began in 403 B.C., when the Eastern Zhou rump court (King Wei Lie) officially recognized Han, Wei, and Zhao, three states that had resulted from the breakup of Jin half a century earlier (453 B.C.). Many scholars, however, accept 475 B.C. as the beginning of the Warring States period, because that year witnessed a dramatic readjustment of the feudal order.

Be that as it may, the Warring States period was in full swing by the beginning of the fourth century B.C., with seven major states (Yan, Qi, Chu, Han, Wei, Zhao, and Qin) contesting for power. The rulers of all of these states usurpingly referred to themselves as "king" (*wang*), and each strove to expand his territory at the expense of the others, with the ultimate goal of achieving complete control over *tianxia* ("all under heaven"). A key feature of the politics of the Warring States period was the ambivalent relationship between a ruler and the feudal lords associated with him. Though the feudal lords may have sworn fealty to the ruler, they were often on the verge of revolting and were constantly trying to assume the dominant position that he occupied. The situation was by nature highly unstable and endlessly in flux, so constant wars were inevitable. These shaky alliances are frequently alluded to in the *Sun Zi*, thus it is essential for the reader to understand them and bear them in mind.

In contrast to the Spring and Autumn period, war during the Warring States period was no longer restricted to brief, chivalrous battles. These had now given way to unrestrained, violent campaigns involving enormous armies. Contributing to the ferocity of warfare during the Warring States were entirely new and ruthlessly efficient military features such as cavalry and the crossbow, both of which appeared in East Asia for the first time during this period (the former from the far north and the latter from the far south), and both of which transformed war into a more terrifying phenomenon than it had ever been before. But the changes in warfare were not restricted to innovations in weaponry and vastly enhanced mobility. The ways in which human beings were marshaled were also thoroughly transformed, with the deployment of mass infantry, the skillful dispatch of spies, and the rise of competing tacticians, none of which had been seen in East Asia before. It was in this highly charged atmosphere that the *Sun Zi* arose.

The hierarchy of organizational levels in the army is alluded to in the *Sun Zi* but not discussed in detail, nor does the *Sun Zi* present a complete listing of the different units of an army and their sizes. The terms referring to the army's manpower that are most frequently mentioned in the *Sun Zi* are the following: *bing* ("soldiers, armed forces"), *zu* ("troops"), *zhong* ("host, crowd"—referring to the army en masse but also sometimes denoting the civilian population upon which the fighting forces of a state depend), and *min* ("the people, populace"—including both the military and the civilian population). It is evident that the authors of the *Sun Zi* were not interested in providing an elaborate organizational scheme for the army, together with normal strengths for each level. Such schemes did exist for the Warring States period (comparable to the corps, brigade, regiment, battalion, company, platoon, squad, and patrol of Western armies), although they varied from state to state and through time. Attention to such specific facets of military administration was not a concern of the authors of the *Sun Zi*, who were preoccupied with more theoretical, political, and psychological aspects of war.

The evolution of the *jiang* or *jiangjun* ("general," i.e., the commander of an army) was another phenomenon of the Warring States period that is reflected prominently in the *Sun Zi*. The first two biographies of generals are both legendary, Sun Wu in *Shi ji* 65 and Marshal Rangju (to whom the *Sima fa* [Methods of the marshal] is attributed) in *Shi ji* 64. Though written around the beginning of the first c. B.C., both biographies were projected back to the waning years of the Spring and Autumn period (late sixth c. B.C.) and both consisted essentially of a single story that emphasized the same principles of military command: absolute adherence to rules, the general as the arbiter of life and death, and the nonnecessity to consult the ruler concerning crucial decisions that had to be made on the battlefield.

Chariots dominated in the warfare of the Spring and Autumn period. The chariot essentially functioned as a movable fighting platform of the elite, supported by loosely organized infantry. The main weapons were the convex bow for the noblemen in their chariots, and the lance for foot soldiers. Armies were relatively small, seldom exceeding 30,000 men and usually much smaller, 10,000 or fewer. The maneuvers that they engaged in, furthermore, were quite simple in nature, and battles seldom lasted more than a day or two, while campaigns were generally limited to at most one season. There was little need for military expertise, with command reserved for members of leading lineages. Nobles led men from their own fiefs, and the armies they constituted functioned essentially as independent units with little overall coordination from a central authority.

As late as the late sixth c. B.C., large armies normally did not exceed 50,000 men. After that, however, there was a pronounced shift toward reliance on massed infantry during the Warring States period, with armies of one or two hundred thousand not uncommon. To fill such vast numbers, rulers had to draw on peasants from the hinterland. They greatly expanded their recruitment, which required enhanced centralized control. Professional commanders gradually replaced noble warrior-leaders. Campaigns could go on for a year or more, with no seasonal limits. Multiple armies could be sent to fight simultaneously in different areas. Weapons proliferated, both in types and quantities. The crossbow, the most important weapon of armies during the latter part of the

Warring States period, did not become widespread until the late fourth c. (Lewis 1999, 2007; Yang Hong 1992:95–98, 2005:79–83, 103–4, 158–64; Zhou Wei 2006 [1957]:97–104). Eventually, the state of Qin, whose ruler in 364 B.C. had already been designated as hegemon (*ba*) or hegemon king (*bawang*, a term that occurs twice in *Sun Zi* 11), one after another subdued all of its rivals. Finally, with the defeat of the great southern state of Chu in 278 and the powerful northern state of Qi in 221, Qin (pronounced like "chin") reunified the empire. In place of the old feudal system that had obtained since the Shang period, the Qin established a political and institutional system of bureaucrats exercising the emperor's will that persisted through a succession of dozens of dynasties until the year 1911. It is no wonder that the largest state of East Asia today is called *China*.

Ironically, this two-century period of incessant war known as the Warring States was the golden age of Chinese thought, when the major philosophical traditions (Confucianism, Taoism, Legalism, and so forth) were founded, the so-called Hundred Schools. It was also the period during which the Chinese writing system was unified and the foundations of Chinese literature were laid. This elicits a conundrum of the highest order: how can it be that a prolonged period of military contestation would result in the most intense intellectual stimulation ever to have occurred in East Asia before modern times? Are there parallels elsewhere? War is a scourge, a blot upon humanity, but for East Asia more than two millennia ago, it induced unforeseen benefits that indelibly shaped one of the world's greatest cultures.

DATING

Tradition holds that the *Sun Zi* was a product of the late Spring and Autumn period, but—judging both from internal and external evidence—this is completely impossible. Everything that the *Sun Zi* has to say about the pattern of war, battle tactics, the conduct of armies, strategic planning, and weaponry is irrelevant to the Spring and Autumn period but perfectly compatible with the Warring States period. The entire modus operandi of warfare as described in the *Sun Zi* pertains to the Warring States and is completely out of keeping with the Spring and Autumn period, when armies were commanded by rulers, members of the aristocracy, vassals, and ministers. It was not until the Warring States period that military professionals of the sort described in the *Sun Zi* took over the job of prosecuting wars. Furthermore, the armies described in the *Sun Zi* are large, well organized, and extensively trained, whereas the armies of the Spring and Autumn period were much smaller, poorly organized, and lacked training. Likewise, the ascription of books to individuals, real or imagined, was a phenomenon of the Warring States, not of Spring and Autumn times. In addition, there are technological innovations mentioned in the *Sun Zi* that disqualify it as a Spring and Autumn text. For example, the crossbow is referred to in chaps. 2, 5, and 11, but it was not common in East Asia until the fourth c. B.C., and probably not known at all until the fifth c. B.C. Warfare during the Warring States period was also transformed by sharp metal weapons made of iron that could be produced on a massive scale, leading to enormous armies. These are just a few of the immediate, insuperable obstacles to the acceptance of the *Sun Zi* as belonging to the Spring and Autumn period.[55] I will raise many more bars to a Spring and Autumn date in the following sections of this introduction, but we already have enough counterevidence to rule out any time before the Warring States for the birth of the *Sun Zi*.

It is clear that the *Sun Zi* belongs to the Warring States, but that does not necessarily imply that it is all of a piece and belongs to a single date within the Warring States period. There are many features of the *Sun Zi* that lead the sensitive, critical reader to the conclusion that, just as it was not all written by the same person, neither was the whole of it written at the same time. Here is a simple chart listing the thirteen chapters of the *Sun Zi* according to their serial order together with the approximate years in which they were composed.[56]

1	309 B.C.
2	311 B.C.
3	312 B.C.
4	313 B.C.
5	314 B.C.
6	316 B.C.
7	317 B.C.
8	336 B.C. (?)
9	345 B.C.
10	342 B.C.
11	330 B.C.
12	310 B.C.
13	272 B.C.

The following list arranges the chapters in their apparent chronological sequence:

345 B.C.	9
342 B.C.	10
336 B.C. (?)	8
330 B.C.	11
317 B.C.	7
316 B.C.	6
314 B.C.	5
313 B.C.	4
312 B.C.	3
311 B.C.	2
310 B.C.	12
309 B.C.	1
272 B.C.	13

What do these dates tell us? First of all, they show that the *Sun Zi* germinated around the middle of the fourth century B.C. with an intense focus on the problem of terrain and the proper positioning of troops in different topographical circumstances. From that concrete, infantry-centered core,[57] the text incrementally grew outward over a span of around thirty-five years to encompass increasingly varied and more abstract, theoretical, and political aspects of war. The main development of the *Sun Zi* concluded, however, toward the end of the fourth century B.C. with a technologically specific chapter on incendiary attacks and a politico-economic tract on planning.[58] Then, after a hiatus of more than a quarter of a century, the *Sun Zi* was brought to a close and co-opted by advocates of the intelligence community.[59]

This general view of the evolution of the thirteen chapters of the *Sun Zi* is corroborated by arranging them in groups according to their content. When this is done, the initial breakdown falls into three groups: 1–6 emphasize basic theory and strategy (the second group to be composed), 7–11 concentrate on tactics and topography (the first group composed), and 12–13 deal with specialized topics (the last group composed). The latter two groups, representing, respectively, the relatively unified core and the periphery furthest removed from it, cannot fruitfully be subdivided. The group in between (time-wise), however, is highly heterogeneous and can be further broken down into 1–3, which concern overall procedures and principles of war making; 4–5, on the intangibles of shape and configuration; and 6, on the most abstract notions of all, emptiness and fullness (or solidity). Finally, 1–3 can, in turn, be subdivided yet again into: 1. prewar assessments, 2. the actual battle in the field, and 3. attacking cities.

STYLISTICS AND STATISTICS

Like many other early texts from the Sinitic realm, the *Sun Zi* possesses overt characteristics marking much of its contents as originally having been orally composed. The most obvious mark of orality is the ubiquitous "Master Sun says" at the beginning of each chapter. Of course, this could be a simulacrum of oral transmission, but at least the compilers felt obliged to make an overt gesture in the direction of oral presentation. There are, however, more deeply embedded features of the *Sun Zi* that mark it as being a collection of orally transmitted aphorisms or "bundled maxims." (Lewis 2005:6)

A peculiar feature of the *Sun Zi* is the remarkably high frequency of the word *gu* ("therefore"), plus its variant *shi gu* ("for this reason"). The character for *gu* occurs 104 times out of a total of 6,692 characters in the *Sun Zi* (Lau 1992:259).[60] This makes it the sixth most frequent character in the entire text, constituting 1.55 percent of all characters in the *Sun Zi*. This is in striking contrast with the frequencies for *gu* observed in other early military texts. See the comparative chart, which helps to put this startling disparity in perspective.[61] This is a phenomenon that may also be observed in the *Tao te ching/Dao de jing*, undoubtedly for similar reasons, namely, the oral background and compilatory nature of the text (Mair 1990:119–26, esp. 123–24).[62] Once a particular genre of written literature (such as the military treatise) is established,

TABLE 1

OCCURRENCES OF *GU* IN FOUR EARLY MILITARY TEXTS

Military Text	Serial Order of *gu*	Total Characters	Occurrences of *gu*	Percentage of *gu* among all characters
Sun Zi	6	6,692	104	1.55
Wei Liao Zi	30	9,484	55	0.58
Wu Zi	53	4,729	18	0.38
Sima fa	49	3,452	14	0.41

subsequent exemplars will have fewer characteristics that evince their derivation from orally transmitted lore.

It is not always possible to say with certainty whether a particular illative[63] conjunction in the *Sun Zi* is genuine or false.[64] As a matter of fact, if one were to apply the most stringent grammatical and logical criteria for the use of illative conjunctions, very few of those in the *Sun Zi* would qualify as genuine. I have, however, given the benefit of the doubt whenever possible (i.e., whenever there is a reasonable connection of any sort between the preceding and succeeding clauses). No matter what degree of rigor is invoked, well over half of the succeeding

TABLE 2

NUMBER OF TRUE AND FALSE ILLATIVE
CONJUNCTIONS PER CHAPTER

Chapter	False	True	Total Illatives	Illatives as a Percentage of All Characters
1	1	3	4	1.18
2	4	2	6	1.74
3	6	3	9	2.1
4	7	3	10	3.24
5	2	3	5	1.5
6	12	1	13	2.15
7	8	6	14	2.94
8	5	0	5	2.02
9	0	1	1	0.16
10	2	4	6	1.1
11	10	3	13	1.21
12	1	2	3	1.06
13	2	4	6	1.28

clauses in the *Sun Zi* manifestly do not follow from the preceding clauses with which they are ostensibly linked by the illative conjunction.

Chapters with a very high proportion of illative conjunctions, especially those with dense concentrations of false illatives (such as chapters 4, 6, 7, and 8), are poorly constructed. Indeed, they tend to read like pastiches of available sayings about war, loosely cobbled together, but given a very thin veneer of logic by artificially linking up the sections with illative conjunctions. In contrast, chapter 9, which has far and away the fewest illative conjunctions (by a factor of about twenty) was most likely the first to be written, thus providing a kernel around which the military-wisdom sayings of the other chapters could crystallize. It is undoubtedly not a coincidence that chapter 9, more than any other chapter in the *Sun Zi*, manifestly presents the appearance of a sustained, closely reasoned, and substantiated argument.

Another striking stylistic feature of the *Sun Zi* is that, except for three chapters (1, 4, and 10), the adverb *fan* ("in general, common[ly], in all cases," etc.) follows immediately after the incipit ("Master Sun said"). What is more, in chapters 2, 3, 7, and 8, right after the *fan* comes *yong bing zhi fa* ("the method of waging war; the method of using military force"), and, at the beginning of chapter 10, this phrase follows on the heels of the incipit, without the interposition of the adverb *fan*. The effect of invoking these universalizing phrases is to claim for Master Sun a type of omniscient military knowledge. Since, however, this is done formulaically, it dilutes the force of the claim, instead becoming a mere mechanical gesture.[65]

The compilatory nature of the *Sun Zi* is plainly evident in the last section of chapter 7, which begins with a false illative clause, "Therefore, the method of engaging in warfare" (lit., "the method of using *bing*"). The section then strings together an assorted series of eight military maxims and concludes lamely with the same hollow clause that began it: "This is the method of engaging in warfare." It is clear that the repeated clause serves little purpose other than as a weak justification for assembling the dicta of sage strategists that were in circulation at the time of the compilation of the text. Furthermore, this final section is not an effective summation of a chapter that is entitled "The Struggle of Armies," a topic which is actually treated only in the first two sections and mentioned again ever so briefly at the close of the third section.

The minimal coherence of the *Sun Zi* may also be seen in the title of chapter 7, "Nine Varieties." This, in itself, is mystifying enough, with commentators at loggerheads over its meaning, and to the extent that the "nine varieties" are discussed at all in the chapter, it is only in the first section. That is followed by five very short sections, each of which begins with a false illative and none of which has anything in particular to do with the title or the first section of the chapter.

The loosely cobbled structure of the *Sun Zi* is evident in many places. Again, for the sake of convenience, we may turn to chapter 7 for a good example, namely, the last sentence of the first section: "This is the planning of one who knows how to make the circuitous straight." When this sentence first appears, it makes good sense because it concludes a discussion on the utilization of circuitousness in dealing with another army. When this sentence is arbitrarily reinserted at the end of a subsequent section of the same chapter, however, it sounds garbled. This sort of slack construction is also revealed in the next sentence ("This is the method of the struggle of armies"), which likewise harkens back to the opening section of the chapter, but not in any coherent, principled way.

Let us now examine a list of the lengths of the various chapters in the *Sun Zi* to see whether we can draw some meaningful conclusions from this data.

LENGTH OF THE INDIVIDUAL CHAPTERS OF THE *SUN ZI*

Chapter no.	No. of characters
1	339
2	345
3	429
4	309
5	337
6	605
7	477
8	248
9	615
10	548
11	1,072
12	283
13	468

Rearranged by size from shortest to longest, the chapters now line up as in the following list.

CHAPTERS OF THE *SUN ZI* ARRANGED ACCORDING TO THEIR LENGTH

No. of characters	Chapter no.
248	8
283	12
309	4
337	5
339	1

345	2
429	3
468	13
477	7
548	10
605	6
615	9
1,072	11

As is evident from these two lists, the chapters of the *Sun Zi* average just over 467 words in length, ranging from a minimum of 248 to a maximum of 1,072. This wide latitude in the size of the chapters suggests different emphases, constituencies, and even authors (a conclusion already arrived at under our consideration of the dating of the various chapters). One of the chapters (11) is disproportionately long and another (8) is markedly shorter than the rest. If we remove these two chapters from our calculations, we find that the average length of a chapter is approximately 432 words per chapter, and the variation from this mean lies roughly between 30 and 40 percent.

Useful inferences can be drawn from these data, such as that the largest chapter is the fourth (and last) in the series of core chapters dealing with matters of topography. This, the eleventh, chapter is also the most poorly integrated of all the chapters, indicating that it served as a sort of summation and grab bag of whatever miscellaneous information remained to be subsumed under the topic of varieties of terrain. Conversely, the penultimate chapter on topography is the shortest in the *Sun Zi* and was probably composed as a sort of afterthought, only serving to elicit its opposite extreme a few years later, viz., chapter 11, which is more than four times as long, but goes over much of the same ground. The next shortest chapter, 12, is also one of the latest and deals with the extraordinary subject of incendiary warfare. The very last chapter, interestingly enough, is almost exactly the length of the average of all the chapters in the book taken together, as though it were consciously designed to strike a balance among all the others, thereby subsuming them under what it proffers as the most important ingredient in the art of war: military intelligence—a topic that was not part of the text as originally conceived by its founding authors, who were primarily interested in how to deploy mass infantry on different types of terrain.

TECHNIQUES AND TECHNOLOGY

Following the waning of the Bronze Age, the appearance of iron during the late second millennium and first millennium B.C. had a thoroughgoing, transformative effect on warfare throughout the world (Keegan 1993:237–98). The steppe-dwelling Scythians appropriated iron metallurgy from its place of origin in the Black Sea region and, together with other Central Asian and Inner Asian peoples, transmitted it all the way across the continent to East Asia.

Iron appears in the East Asian Heartland (hereafter EAH) from ca. 500 B.C. It is very rare at first (during the latter part of the Spring and Autumn period) and restricted almost entirely to the northern fringes of the region. By the early Warring States, there was a vast inventory of iron tools and weapons along the northern borderlands of the EAH. Attempts have been made to demonstrate an autochthonous origin for iron making in the southeastern states of Wu and Yue, but they are not supported by present evidence, since very few iron objects have been found in the lower Yangtze region, and none preceding the end of the sixth c. B.C. In contrast, there is abundant evidence of iron tools and weapons all along the northern and northwestern fringes of the EAH well before this time, strongly suggesting a western origin for siderurgy (iron technology).

Indeed, ferrous metallurgy spread in the north(west)ern zone before its appearance in the EAH, with iron objects having been recovered from Scytho-Siberian sites in the Altai (Eastern Central Asia) dating to the ninth c. B.C. and in what is now Inner Mongolia no later than the mid-seventh c. B.C. There is evidence for iron along the Amur River already by the end of the second millennium B.C., and iron objects have been found at many sites in Central Asia by the beginning of the first millennium B.C. Subsequently, iron artifacts (many of them horse-related, but also weapons, belt ornaments, and tools) became more common in the nearer northwest (the Ordos, Ningxia, Gansu), indicating a vector of introduction by nomads coming down off the steppe. Such a south(east)ward trajectory through the Gansu Corridor and the Ordos, the omphalos of eastern Eurasia (Mair 2005a:79–82), is in conformity with the overall chronology and geography of the spread of iron technology from its center near the Black Sea starting around 3,200 years ago.[66] In any event, a large-scale iron industry did not develop in East Asia itself until the Warring States, and it is my opinion that the advent of iron was one of the main factors that precipitated the radical political and societal adjustments that characterized the region during this tumultuous period (Hua, Yang, and Liu 1960; Dubs 1947:82n. 121; Needham 1964; Tang 1993; Bagley 1999:177n. 80; Rawson 1999:400n. 68; Lewis 1999:624–25; Falkenhausen 1999:475n. 31, 534–37n. 157, 542; 2006:3n. 4, 9, 224, 227, 229, 282, 409–10, 412; and, most importantly, Di Cosmo 1999:891–92, 913–14, 933, 938, 940, 946–47, 953, 956, 959).

The impact of iron grew as its production gradually became less restricted, but the full military effect of the Iron Revolution was not felt in East Asia until the fourth and third centuries B.C. By that time, it was possible to produce sharp, hard weapons in quantity for distribution to large bodies of infantry. The mass production of quality iron weapons, which was not possible using bronze because the copper and tin ores needed to make it are rarer, changed the nature of war. It is precisely at this moment that the feudal institutions that had been in place since the second millennium yielded to bureaucratic institutions (Mair 1990a:160–61). Axiomatically, we may state that bronze is to feudalism as iron is to the bureaucratic state.

Bronze weapons had been brought to East Asia from Central Asia and West Asia a thousand years earlier than iron, causing tremendous transformations of society and state (Loehr 1956; An 1993).[67] The bronze weapons were probably introduced by the same Iranian-speaking peoples who brought the chariot (Shaughnessy 1988, 1989; Anthony 2007; Kuzmina 2007) and the horse (Mair 2003; Mallory and Mair 2000), curiously paralleling the role of the Scythians and other Iranian-speaking peoples in the transmission of iron technology. The Iron Revolution in East Asia, however, resulted in even more profoundly convulsive changes than had the Bronze Revolution, because it reached further down into and more broadly across society. Whereas the limited supply of bronze weapons meant that they were perforce restricted to elite warriors, iron could be put into the hands of the plebs en masse.

Another major technological advance in warfare during the Warring States period was the invention of the crossbow in Southeast Asia and its infiltration northward. The crossbow is employed for metaphorical purposes both in *Sun Zi* and in *Sun Bin,* rather than having its military usage explained. In *Sun Zi* 5, there is a discussion of *shi* ("configuration") that draws an analogy with a bird of prey ready to spring or the trigger of a crossbow ready to fire. *Sun Bin* 9, also in a discussion of *shi,* begins with similar, but much more elaborate animal imagery and also touches on swords, boats, chariots, and a long-handled weapon—each employed as a metaphor for some aspect of military *sagesse,* not with regard to their actual use in combat. *Sun Bin* 10 presents an even more elaborate metaphor involving the crossbow, again, though, without regard for how to use it in battle.[68]

After iron, the most important Warring States innovation in military affairs was the ridden house. Cavalry was introduced into the EAH around the mid-fourth c. B.C. in emulation of north(west)ern peoples (Mair 2006, 2005a, 2003; Dubs 1947). Cavalry figures prominently in *Sun Bin,* e.g., chapter 7 and chapter 18, and especially in a passage recovered from Du You's encyclopedia that discusses ten advantages of using cavalry and is explicitly assigned to Sun Bin (Lau and Ames 2003:179, 235n. 383), all of which demonstrate that Sun Bin was quite familiar with cavalry, but such is not at all the case in *Sun Zi.*[69] Therefore *Sun Zi* must have been put together largely before the introduction of cavalry, and *Sun Bin* shortly thereafter. In other words, cavalry constitutes the *terminus ad quem* for the *Sun Zi* and the *terminus a quo* of the *Sun Bin.*

It is conceivable that one might argue for an early date of the *Sun Zi* solely on the basis of its lack of any mention of cavalry. After all, it is true that the states of the EAH certainly were unfamiliar with mounted warfare during the Spring and Autumn period. But that would be to ignore all of the other internal and external evidence for the *Sun Zi* as a product of the Warring States period. The northern states of the EAH did not adopt cavalry from the north(west)ern nomads till the latter part of the fourth c. B.C. By that time all but the conspicuously late chapter of the *Sun Zi* on espionage had been brought together. Furthermore, it was not until still later that this new technique of warfare passed to the south, where the *Sun Zi* was ostensibly written (the southeastern state of Wu).[70]

Cavalry in East Asia always played only a supporting role and never became a major force within the army. It was used for skirmishing, reconnaissance, ambushes, and raids (*qí* applications)—not in main battle (*zheng* operations). Because of the terrain and the environment, the mounted horse was never a key feature of warfare in East Asia. Furthermore, East Asians always had a strained relationship with the horse, which was not in its natural element (that, above all, was the steppe). Nevertheless, it was a prestige item, like the chariot (Mair 2006).

There is not a single reference to cavalry in the whole of the thirteen chapters of the received text of the *Sun Zi*. Horses are mentioned three times in the *Sun Zi* (chaps. 2, 9, and 11), but only for purposes of chariot traction. Some passages from later encyclopedias that have been attributed to the *Sun Zi* do mention cavalry, but it would be better to assign these to the *Sun Bin,* since the authors of the latter text were clearly aware of mounted warfare, whereas there is no evidence that the compilers of the *Sun Zi* knew much, if anything, about it. Cavalry was first introduced to a state of the EAH near the end of the fourth c. B.C. To be more precise, this happened in the year 307, when King Wuling of Zhao commanded a portion of his men to adopt nomadic dress (pants and jacket or shirt instead of robes) and learn to ride horses so that they could resist the mobile nomad warriors of the steppe (Mair 2003:174ab). Zhao, however, was a northern state, so an experiment with cavalry there would have necessitated a lag time before this new skill was passed to states further south. Thus we may posit the end of the fourth c. as a rough *terminus ad quem* for the compilation of the *Sun Zi* (excepting the anomalous chap. 13, on spies, which must have been added on after a considerably long interval—perhaps as much as a quarter of a century—had expired from the time when the last previous chapter was appended).

As for a *terminus a quo* for the compilation of the *Sun Zi,* I have adduced numerous specific features that certify it as post–Spring and Autumn. This means that its compilation must have begun sometime after the first quarter of the fifth c. B.C., which is when the Warring States period commenced. Various specific criteria (the crossbow, mass infantry forces, etc.) mark the text as belonging to the fourth c. or later.

Defensive walls, both external and internal, were also a significant factor during the Warring States period. Qin linked up the earlier walls of Zhao, Yan, and the ones they had constructed themselves to form the forerunner of what is now known as the Great Wall (Waldron 1990). Walled cities are mentioned in the *Sun Zi*, but precedents for them had already been present in the EAH since prehistoric times, when settlements were often surrounded by rammed-earth fortifications. Territorial defensive walls, though an important development in Warring States times, are not explicitly integrated in the strategy of the *Sun Zi*. They would, however, have implicitly affected the tactics advocated by its authors.

EURASIAN PARALLELS

Among the works collected by the followers of the great altruistic philosopher Master Mo (ca. 468–376 B.C.),[71] under the title *Mo Zi*, there are twenty chapters (52–71 [only eleven of which survive]) dealing with defensive warfare. Together they form section 5, the last portion of the work,[72] and they are all concerned with how to defend a city. Some of these chapters respond directly to types of attacks mentioned in the *Sun Zi*. For example, chapter 63 of the *Mo Zi* is entitled "Bei 'yi fu'" (Preparing against the "ant approach," i.e., swarming up walls), which is specifically referred to in *Sun Zi*, chapter 3. *Mo Zi*, chapter 58, "Bei shui" (Preparing against water) is directed against the sort of hydraulic attacks that are briefly mentioned in *Sun Zi*, chapter 12. Among the missing chapters of the last section of the *Mo Zi*, there certainly would have been one entitled "Bei huo" (Preparing against fire), the type of attack vigorously promoted in *Sun Zi*, chapter 12. The concern of another late chapter of the *Mo Zi*, chapter 62, "Bei xue" (Preparing against tunneling), which probably dated to around 300 B.C., is not specifically mentioned in the late chapters of the *Sun Zi*, such as chapter 3 and chapter 12, but it is also directly related to the type of siegecraft with which they are concerned (Yates 1982, 1988, 1980).

It would appear that the authors of these late chapters of the *Mo Zi* and the authors of the corresponding chapters of the *Sun Zi* (also late) must have been in some sort of dialogic relationship with one another. Judging from specific textual evidence, furthermore, it would appear that the *Mo Zi*–*Sun Zi* tradition of siegecraft and defense against it developed in tandem with Greco-Roman tactics and military science.

There is a perfect Greek word for all of these devices employed in the siege of cities, namely, poliorcetics, so one would expect that such techniques and technologies would have been well developed by the ancient Greeks. Such, indeed, is the case, starting with the celebrated attack on Troy that "stands at the beginning of Greek history and literature and has captured the imagination of poets and antiquarians, the mighty and the common people, from its conclusion towards the end of the second millennium B.C. down to modern times" (Needham and Yates 1994:241).

Although much has been lost from the canon of Greco-Roman military writing,[73] we are extremely fortunate to have portions of the military writings of Aineias the Tactician.[74] By sheer good luck, the largest segment of the work of Aineias to survive is his chapters on how to survive under siege, which precisely mirror the military chapters of the *Mo Zi*. Internal evidence dates the anti-poliorcetic chapters of Aineias to ca. 355–350 B.C. This puts them before (but still in the same timeframe as) the late chapters of the *Mo Zi* and the *Sun Zi* that are concerned with siegecraft and defense against it.

The parallels between the chapters of Aineias on how a city should defend itself against sieges and the chapters of the *Mo Zi* on exactly the same subject are so numerous, so detailed, and so close—even in the most extraordinary, uncanny details—that it would seem virtually impossible that they could have arisen entirely independently. For instance, both describe the construction of similar mechanical devices to raise, transport, and release projectiles and weapons against the enemy; both advocate the digging of counter-tunnels against the tunneling of attackers; both specify the use of geophones to detect tunneling by the enemy;[75] both discuss the employment of asphyxiating materials and devote attention to means for channeling smoke toward the enemy; both emphasize the importance of vinegar for protective purposes;[76] both stress the need to plate the bolt (cross-bar) of the gate with iron; both explain the use of the portcullis; both enjoin the secure tethering of dogs; both emphasize measures for dealing with ladders placed against the wall; and so forth. There are countless points of comparison between Aineias and the *Mo Zi*, such that it would be futile to catalog all of them. Yet, when we consider that nearly half of the military chapters of the *Mo Zi* are lost and that several of those that do survive are fragmentary, plus the fact that we have only a very small proportion of Aineias' oeuvre,[77] the resonances between the two complete texts would surely have been far greater than they appear under the present conditions. In comparison with the military writings of Aineias and the military chapters of the *Mo Zi*, the *Sun Zi* is terse and unconcerned with the sort of practical, mundane minutiae that preoccupy them. Still, echoes of a common military heritage may be heard even in our slender text.

By no means am I suggesting that there necessarily was a direct connection between the *Mo Zi* or the *Sun Zi* and Aineias' work. Indeed, there were other early Greek tacticians whose writings have disappeared, and there may well have been intermediaries involved. What I do believe is that, during this Axial Age, military wisdom, as so many other aspects of culture, was a product of the human ecumene. This is not to assert that there was only a single Eurasian military culture, for it is clear that local traditions were strong and distinctive. On the other hand, the common aspects should not be ignored when they do occur.

A few of the features shared between the Greco-Roman tradition of military tactics and Warring States military practices have been highlighted above. Obviously, there were significant differences as well. For example, although both emphasize the importance of signals and messages, Aineias goes into great detail about alphabetic writing, including ways to encode it, whereas the *Mo Zi* scarcely mentions writing at all, except for names. Another salient distinction between the two traditions is the plethora of illustrative examples drawn from earlier battles in history and copious extracts from previous writers, a standard feature of European works such as Aineias' *Tactics* (ca. 350 B.C.), Frontinus' *Strategemata* (first c. A.D.), Polyaenus' *Strategemata* (first c. A.D.), and Flavius Vegetius Renatus' *Epitome rei militaris* (384–395 A.D.), versus their virtually complete absence in Warring States works such as the *Mo Zi* and the *Sun Zi*, making the latter seem as though they were operating in a historical vacuum. Conversely, the *Mo Zi* goes into greater technical detail concerning the size, dimensions, construction, and quantity of the devices and structures it describes, whereas Aineias is generally content to provide brief, schematic descriptions.[78] Finally, the *Mo Zi* makes reference to certain technical innovations that are absent in Aineias' chapters, namely crossbows, bellows, and well-sweeps (though the "swing-beams" mentioned by Aineias would have fulfilled a similar function).[79]

In discussing the environment in which Aineias wrote his *Tactics*, David Whitehead (Aineias 1990:34) offers a clue toward understanding the circumstances under which the *Sun Zi* may have evolved from a body of orally circulating lore into a written text:

> It seems to have been in the last third of the fifth century—in other words, during the Peloponnesian War [431–404 B.C.]— that military expertise began to evolve from its origins as a

loose-knit body of traditional wisdom and experience, passed on from father to son where it could not be absorbed from reading or listening to Homer, into a technical subject, a branch of formal education taught by sophists and other self-styled experts.

The motivation for writing down the collected maxims of the *Sun Zi* during the pervasive militarism of the Warring States period would have been similar.

The continuities in Eurasian military tactics and techniques during the fourth c. B.C. were by no means limited to East Asia and Europe.[80] A celebrated Sanskrit work entitled the *Arthaśāstra* (Treatise on material well-being),[81] essentially a manual of the science of politics and administration, has numerous chapters on warfare. The authorship of the *Arthaśāstra* is traditionally ascribed to Kauṭilya, who placed Candragupta Maurya on the throne of Magadha in 321 B.C. Since the *Arthaśāstra* was meant to be a handbook of government for the new ruler, it follows that it would have been written in the latter part of the fourth c. B.C., placing it about half a century after the *Tactics* of Aineias and roughly the same amount of time before the *Sun Zi* and the military chapters of the *Mo Zi*.[82]

All together there are fifteen books in the *Arthaśāstra*, which are divided into 180 sections. One-third of the books and more than two-fifths of all the sections have to do with various aspects of war. What is more, many of the subjects discussed in the sections of the *Arthaśāstra* devoted to war are held in common with Aineias, the *Sun Zi*, and the military chapters of the *Mo Zi*: incendiary attacks, siegecraft, deception, terrain, arrangement of troops, espionage, and so on.[83] In particular, the use of various types of secret agents and secret practices is advocated in numerous places throughout the *Arthaśāstra*, which resonates perfectly with *Sun Zi* 13.

TAOISTIC ASPECTS

It may seem odd that the *Sun Zi* is included in the Taoist canon—not once, but twice! These two editions are the *Sun Zi zhujie* (Commentaries on the Sun Zi), which is essentially the same edition as the *Shiyi jia zhu Sun Zi* described above, and the *Sun Zi yishuo* (Gleanings from the Sun Zi), whose late-eleventh- or early-twelfth-century editor, Zheng Youxian, employs fictitious dialog to underscore what he sees as the philosophical depth of the text.[84] What is a treatise on war doing in a collection of supposedly religious texts? Aside from the fact that there are many other works in the Taoist canon that can hardly be described as religious in nature, let us proceed on the assumption that whoever was responsible for welcoming the *Sun Zi* into the Taoist canon had a reason for doing so and see whether there is indeed an affinity between the *Sun Zi* and Taoism.

The *Sun Zi* constitutes what may be thought of as a Taoistic approach to war (Rand 1979–1980). Its authors manifestly recognized that a country sometimes must go to war to protect its own interests, perhaps even to ensure its very survival. In their eyes, war is a matter of last resort, and it should be undertaken with the least effort, least expenditure, least risk, and least loss of life. In short, the *Sun Zi*'s approach to war is minimalist.

The *Sun Zi* advocates adherence to the Way (Tao/Dao) as the chief criterion for victory in battle. But what exactly is the Way as applied to warfare? In the very first chapter, Master Sun tells us that the Way (of warfare) is to cause the people to share the same sentiments (be of one mind) with their superiors. It is striking that a work of military theory would begin with such a blatantly political statement, but this is very much in the manner of Lao Zi: rely on the Way to rule the world.

The other key term of the title of the *Tao te ching/Dao de jing*, namely *te* or *de* (*virtūs*, "virtue," but in the original Latin sense of "manliness," "excellence of character," "valor," "worth" < *vir* ["man"]) is completely missing from the *Sun Zi*. As a matter of fact, *de* is important both for Taoists and for Confucians, though with different emphases (Mair 1990:133–35; Zhang 2002:337–44). For the Taoists, *de* was the immanence of the Tao in the individual, a kind of charismatic power. For the Confucians, *de* was an ethical concept akin to goodness. In the *Sun Zi*, though, *de* drew a blank.

Master Sun's attitudes toward the prosecution of war were very different from those of contemporary Confucians. In the chapter of the *Li ji* (Records of ritual) entitled "Zhong Ni yan ju" (When Confucius was dwelling in retirement), it is stated that "The army has *li* [civility, etiquette, ritual, propriety], therefore it accomplishes military merit." Under the fourteenth year of Duke Ai (481 B.C.) of the *Zuo zhuan* (Chronicle of Zuo; completed ca. 312), it is claimed that "Having *li*, there will be no defeat." The *Sun Zi* does not mention *li* even once. In thus ignoring the prime Confucian virtue of *li*, Master Sun is very much in agreement with the early Taoist thinkers who considered reliance on it to be a hypocritical form of behavior and a cause of dishonesty in human interactions.

Though the *Sun Zi* may have been estranged from Confucianism, it gives every appearance of having arisen more or less in concert with the *Dao de jing* during the mid- to late fourth century B.C. Both texts were projected back in time to ahistorical authors who were imagined to have lived approximately two centuries earlier, during the late Spring and Autumn period. The *Sun Zi* consists of military aphorisms attributed to a hazy, legendary figure, just as the *Dao de jing* is a collection of mystical maxims grouped around a vague, semidivine founder, the Old Master (Mair 1990a:119–30).

That the second half of the fourth century B.C. was indeed the time during which the *Dao de jing* was transformed from a body of orally circulating maxims into a written text found "startling" confirmation in 1993 with the archeological recovery of bamboo strip manuscripts at Guodian (Hubei Province, east central China). Dating to around 300 B.C. and published in 1998, these astonishing manuscripts reveal a *Dao de jing* in process of formation. As had long been suspected by rigorously critical scholars on diverse grounds, the Guodian manuscripts provide convincing evidence that the *Dao de jing* was the product of multiple authors and editors over a considerable period of time instead of the work of a single individual writing during the latter part of the Spring and Autumn period (the traditional view) (Henricks 2000).[85]

Precisely the same conditions obtain for the *Sun Zi*. Traditionally held to be the work of a man called Sun Wu who was supposedly a late–Spring and Autumn period contemporary of Confucius, modern critical scholarship (confirmed by seemingly miraculous but wonderfully palpable manuscript finds) has demonstrated conclusively that the *Sun Zi* emerged during the second half of the fourth century and that it incorporates the collective, aphoristic wisdom of the age. The chief difference between the *Dao de jing* and the *Sun Zi* is that the former focuses on how to use a *wuwei* ("nonaction") approach to rule a state, whereas the latter concentrates on applying a similar attitude toward the prosecution of war.[86] (Mair 1990:138) The supremely adept general is the one who could subdue the enemy without fighting. Thus the *Dao de jing* is a manual for the *wuwei*-minded ruler, and the *Sun Zi* is a handbook for the *wuwei*-minded general.[87]

Finally, I note that at least one version of the *Sun Zi* in sixteen chapters was classified by Han Dynasty bibliographers as belonging to the Taoist School (*daojia*).[88]

ON THE WORLD STAGE

Abroad, the *Sun Zi* has received widespread recognition, with translations into Japanese, French, Russian, German, English, and many other languages. The first known translation of the *Sun Zi*, however, was into Tangut, an extinct Tibeto-Burman (more precisely Qiangic-Tibetan) language. The Tanguts ruled over a large, powerful state extending from Mongolia to Eastern Central Asia. This state was referred to in Chinese as Xi Xia ("Western Xia") (1038–1227 [destroyed by Genghis Khan]).[89]

The Tangut translation of the *Sun Zi* is preserved in a unique block print of the twelfth c.[90] The Tangut text includes commentaries by Cao Cao, Li Quan, and Du Mu. The parts of the fragmentary woodblock-printed text that remain are chapters 7 through 11, 13, and the biography of Sun Zi. There are not many discrepancies between extant Chinese texts of the *Sun Zi* and the Tangut translation, which means that the *Sun Zi* must have become fairly stable by the Song period. The main differences are in the wording of the commentaries. The exact Chinese edition of the *Sun Zi* that served as the original for the Tangut translation no longer exists. Nonetheless, it is still possible to correlate portions of the Tangut translation with corresponding passages of the received Chinese text. For instance, where the Chinese text reads, "If the enemy is profligate in handing out rewards, it means that he is in extremity," the Tangut version has "[If the general] often gives rewards, [that is be]cause [his] troops find themselves in a position from which they cannot escape" (26b, 1.1; Keping 1979; Huang 1992). The Tangut version includes a total of approximately 1,200 different characters, nearly twice as many as in the Chinese version (around 700 different characters), a reflection of the monumentally complicated script in which it was written.

The next translation of the *Sun Zi* into an Asian language was into Japanese, entitled *Sonshi kokujikai,* which was completed around 1750 by Butsu Mokei (Ogyū Sorai, 1666–1728) and published in Kyoto by the monastery called Izumoji. After that, there were numerous other editions and translations of the *Sun Zi* in Japan, the earliest consisting basically of the Chinese text with marks directing the reader how to rearrange and pronounce the characters. It was only in the twentieth century that translations of the *Sun Zi* into modern Japanese began to appear. Of the many that are available, some with copious annotations, I have consulted those by Amano Shizuo (1972), Asano Yuichi (1986), Murayama Yoshihiro (in Kanaya Osamu et al. [1973]), and Yamai Yū (1975).

It is not surprising that the rulers of the Qing Dynasty (1644–1911) would have ensured that there be a translation into their native tongue, Manchu. The Manchu themselves were superb military rulers, and they studied the *Sun Zi* very carefully to understand the military thinking of their Sinitic subjects. This is perhaps the most authoritative of translations, because it was done by people who were perfectly bilingual and who were thoroughly familiar with Chinese practices.[91]

The first translation of the *Sun Zi* into a European language was into French, produced by the Jesuit missionary Jean Joseph Marie Amiot (February 8, 1718 [Toulon]–October 8/9, 1793 [Peking]). Amiot went to China in 1750 and became the confidant of the Qianlong emperor (r. 1736–1795). He stayed in China for forty-three years, until his death in 1793. Amiot's translation of the *Sun Zi* appeared in 1772 and was republished in 1782. This was a start, but left much to be desired in that it mixed commentary and the translator's own ideas in with the text.

The next translation into a European language was into English, by Everard Ferguson Calthrop (1876–1915), a British army language student, which appeared in 1905. First issued in Japan, it refers to Sun Zi by the Japanese pronunciation, Sonshi. Although the translation of Calthrop was lacking in fidelity to the original (which is, after all, fraught with difficult philological problems), it joined Amiot's French version in marking the beginning of European exposure to East Asian military thinking. During the last century, scores of translations of the *Sun Zi* have been published in

European and other languages, making it second to the *Dao de jing* in popularity among Chinese texts circulating outside of China. At some point in the twentieth century, the rumor was floated that Napoleon had read Amiot's translation of the *Sun Zi*. As time passed, the rumor grew into a legend that had Napoleon carefully studying the *Sun Zi,* carrying it on his campaigns, and being heavily influenced by it. It is a romantic story, one designed to capture the imagination, but the entire legend is sheer fabrication and easily debunked. In the first place, no one has ever pointed to a single Napoleonic battle that evinces Master Sun's influence. Still more damning is the fact that Napoleon (1769–1821) would have been only three years old when Amiot's French translation of the *Sun Zi* was published, and although there was some notice of Amiot's translation in French literary journals when it was first published in 1772, the book soon dropped out of sight so far as the general public was concerned, becoming a matter of interest chiefly to a handful of Sinologists.[92] What is more, Napoleon made it unmistakably clear who his military mentors were:

> Peruse again and again the campaigns of Alexander, Hannibal, Caesar, Gustavus Adolphus, Turennne, Eugene, and Frederick. Model yourself upon them. This is the only means of becoming a great captain, and of acquiring the secret of the art of war. Your own genius will be enlightened and improved by this study, and you will learn to reject all maxims foreign to the principles of these great commanders.
>
> (Napoleon 2004:80, maxim 78)

It is unlikely that Napoleon, who strongly adhered to this principle of learning from the concrete battlefield experiences of the great generals of the past, would have put much stock in the generalized recommendations of the *Sun Zi.*

More recently, *Sun Zi* partisans have surmised that the Nazi High Command may have consulted the ancient oriental oracle, but the evidence in favor of this supposition is even flimsier than that for Napoleon's alleged attraction to the *Sun Zi*. By deflating these unsubstantiated claims, I do not mean to diminish the *Sun Zi*'s place in history, only to delineate it as accurately as possible. Both the Napoleonic French and the Nazi Germans were far more Clausewitzian than to be influenced by an impressionistic, aphoristic text like the *Sun Zi*. Indeed, in terms of the principles adduced in it, the *Sun Zi* more nearly resembles Machiavelli's *Art of War* than the highly systematic *On War* of Clausewitz.

What, then, were the chief contributions of the *Sun Zi*? First of all, Master Sun pointed out the universal rule of military engagement that, if one knows oneself and one's opponent, one will not be vanquished even in a hundred battles (chap. 3 n. 9; chap. 10 n. 4). Mao Zedong (1893–1976), chairman of the Chinese Communist Party and of the People's Republic of China, placed great value upon this famous dictum from the *Sun Zi*, according it the status of a "scientific truth" (*kexue de zhenli*).[93]

Another major feature of Master Sun's strategy is his emphasis on flexibility. One should be ready to change plans in accordance with actual circumstances. If, for example, the enemy shows himself to be vulnerable in a certain place, attack him there instead of according to some blueprint drawn up ahead of time. At the same time, one should avoid revealing any particular weak spots for one's foe to attack.

A key concept of the *Sun Zi* is that success in war is very much a matter of deception. Deceiving one's enemy is like making a feint in soccer, basketball, or football. One leads his opponent to think that he is preparing to make a certain move or go in a certain direction, then immediately shifts and does something else entirely different.

In general, the *Sun Zi*'s approach to warfare is motivated by the desire to achieve practical results (in simplest terms, victory over one's opponent), not by abstract principles, historical considerations, or spiritual qualms. As such, the *Sun Zi* has valuable advice to offer anyone who is engaged in conflict with an intransigent foe. On the other hand, there are many limitations to the approach advocated in the *Sun Zi*. For example, it is not always possible to achieve a swift victory; thus Master Sun's distaste for prolonged war may lead an impatient general into difficulties that might be avoided by a more deliberate approach. Master Sun's overwhelming desire to subdue his opponents without actually fighting may also sometimes be self-defeating, especially when faced with a highly aggressive, powerful, and competent opponent. Finally, Master Sun overemphasized the uniquely decisive role of the commander. One gains very little sense of the development of a corps of capable officers or the elaboration of a reliable chain of command—both of which are essential when managing large armies.

At the heart of the *Sun Zi* is a "gradualist military strategy" (Keegan 1993:202). The authors of the *Sun Zi* claim that they are against prolonged war, but what they are really opposed to is a war of attrition. They do not mind a long, drawn-out war, so long as it is not costly. This is very different from the contemporary doctrine of Rapid Dominance with its principles of "overwhelming decisive force" and "spectacular displays of power" (also called "shock and awe"), which tend to be stupendously expensive. In war, sometimes it is necessary to be content with patient, incremental gains. Maybe there is something to be said for a strategy that ingeniously combines both approaches (first Clausewitz, then Sun Zi).

In sum, the fundamental lesson that the *Sun Zi* teaches is to go to war only as a last resort. Furthermore, if you must fight, get it over with as quickly as possible and with the least possible loss of life and waste of resources. As recommended in chapter 3, one should avoid combat whenever possible by resorting to political and diplomatic means. Hence, the brave warrior and celebrated hero of Greek and Roman civilization were not exalted in Chinese culture, where warfare was looked upon as a matter of "no alternative," not an opportunity for glory (Loewe 1999:1020). Neither is honor a part of the picture for Master Sun and his epigones, only winning—not at all possible costs, but with the least possible expense. The *Sun Zi* represents the distillation of the military wisdom of a war-plagued, war-weary era. Even though we do not know who its authors were, this little volume still merits the most careful consideration, not just in war but in daily life. There are many reasons for the surge in popularity of the *Sun Zi,* including China's overall rise to prominence in the global economy and world affairs. More intrinsically, however, it offers valuable lessons for businesspeople and for individuals interested in personal development. Everyone has his or her foes, and the *Sun Zi* teaches effective means for dealing with them.

Notes

1. There are other titles by which the *Sun Zi* sometimes goes, including *Wú Sun Zi (bingfa),* not to be confused with the *Wú Zi* (which will be discussed extensively below under the rubric of "Authorship"), and *Sun Wǔ bingfa.* It would be tedious to list all the titles and editions by which this famous book of strategy has been known throughout history.

2. Other common renderings of *bingfa* are "art of war" and "methods of war." As an alternative, I would like to suggest "soldierly methods," stressing that the word *bing* means primarily "weapons" and the men who wield weapons, i.e., "soldiers." Furthermore, "soldier" has a range of meanings, all of which may be encompassed in the expression "soldierly methods":

1. A person who serves in an army; a person engaged in military service
2. An enlisted man or woman, as distinguished from a commissioned officer: *the soldiers' mess and the officers' mess*
3. A person of military skill or experience: *George Washington was a great soldier*
4. A person who contends or serves in any cause; *a soldier of the Lord*

As for "soldierly," it is simply the adjectival form of "soldier," and it has been in our language since the 1570s (*RH*, s.v.).

3. For a valuable introduction to the history of warfare in China, see Kierman and Fairbank (1974). Although the book oddly skips over the Warring States period, it affords a good macro- and micro-exposure to Chinese ways in war. The first chapter by Fairbank is particularly insightful in assessing the distinction and interplay between *wen* ("civil") and *wu* ("martial"), the bureaucratic containment of militarism, and the importance of Central and Inner Asia for China's military history. For the intellectual history of early Chinese military theorists, see Rand (1977). For a bibliographically rich research guide to the history of war in China, see Wilkinson (2000), section 28, pp. 554–64.

4. When there are shared resemblances among the early military treatises, it is by no means assured which way the influence is flowing. In fact, in many cases, the congruencies may be due to borrowing from a lost source such as the *Jun zhi* or *Jun zheng*, or from a common reservoir of orally transmitted military lore.

5. See appendix, n. 5.

6. The "Yiwen zhi" (Treatise on literature), a cumulative bibliography that forms part of the *Han shu* (History of the Western Han Dynasty), lists fifty-three manuals of warfare that were known to exist in the first century B.C. Among them is a *Wú Sun Zi bingfa* (Military methods of Master Sun of the state of Wú) in eighty-two chapters (*pian*) with nine scrolls of illustrations (*tu jiu juan*). The "Yiwen zhi" also lists, among the works of the Taoist School (*daojia*) a *Sun Zi* in sixteen chapters. In addition, it is noteworthy that the "Yiwen zhi" lists a *Qi Sun Zi* (*Sun Zi* of the state of Qi) in eighty-nine scrolls

plus four scrolls of illustrations. This is probably a recension of the same work that is known as the *Sun Bin bingfa*. It is evident that, during the first century B.C., not only was there a plentiful supply of military treatises for readers to choose from, the number that were called *Sun Zi* of one sort or another reveals a corpus that was still fluid and expanding.

7. The *Shiyi jia zhu Sun Zi* has been reissued in a handy new format under the title *Shiyi jia zhu Sun Zi jiaoli*, for which see the bibliography under Yang Bing'an (1999).

8. Du You was not originally included in the list of the ten main commentators on the *Sun Zi* because he had not written a separate commentary on the text. Rather, in compiling the *Tongdian*, he commented extensively on the *Sun Zi*, and his remarks were extracted to form the eleventh member of the expanded *Shiyi jia zhu Sun Zi*.

9. In the notes to the translation, examples of annotations by all of the eleven main commentators on the *Sun Zi* are given. Such annotations are almost never useful, much less definitive, for solving difficult philological problems in the text, but they do give insight into how military specialists from later centuries interpreted the *Sun Zi*, and sometimes they are downright charming.

10. A succinct treatment of the textual and commentarial history of the *Sun Zi* is available in Gawlikowski and Loewe (1993).

11. These seven military classics were assembled at the request of the Song emperor Shenzong (r. 1068–1085) and presented to him by the compilers in 1080. A complete, annotated translation of all seven works is available in Sawyer (1993).

12. There are slight discrepancies between the received text as preserved in the *Shiyi jia zhu Sun Zi* and in the *Wu jing qi shu*, particularly in chapter 9.

13. The Chinese texts are transcribed in Yinque Shan Hanmu zhujian zhengli xiaozu (1976:94–111) and their English translations are available in Ames (1993:173–96). The significance of these tomb texts in the history of writings on military matters is discussed in Lewis (2005). It is essential to note, however, that none of these five Yinque Shan texts that have been assigned by modern editors to

the *Sun Zi* corpus mentions Sun Wu by name, only Sun Zi ("Master Sun"), although the first and the fifth adopt the simulacrum of interviews with the king of Wu (with the fifth specifically mentioning Helu), hence they can be ascribed to the emerging (but not yet fully formed) legend of Sun Wu as military adviser to the king of Wu. The second, third, and fourth texts might just as well have been assigned to the Sun Bin corpus, or simply left to an indeterminate "Master Sun" body of military lore.

In contrast, while the Yinque Shan texts that have been assigned by modern editors to the Sun Bin corpus do not mention Sun Bin by name either (he is always called just Sun Zi ["Master Sun"]), they possess a higher degree of historical specificity. The *Sun Bin* fragments refer to particular battles and the individuals who participated in them, together with the number of troops involved and the movements made. In this regard, they are more like Western (Greco-Roman) military treatises than is the *Sun Zi* and its associated fragments.

The notion of a fixed formation is more prominent in the *Sun Bin* than in the *Sun Zi*, which is another difference between the two, just as is the greater emphasis in the *Sun Zi* on assessment and planning than in the *Sun Bin*. On the other hand, both the *Sun Zi* and the *Sun Bin* have dialogic (especially questions [from a ruler] and answers [from the military specialist]) chapters.

The Yinque Shan manuscripts have made it crystal clear that, by the second half of the second century B.C., there were two separate Sun Zi traditions, one focused on Sun Wu as a military adviser in the southern state of Wu and the other focused on Sun Bin as a military adviser in the northern state of Qi. What is not so clear is how to classify the indeterminate Sun Zi materials from manuscript finds and recovered from later encyclopedias that do not fall unmistakably into either the Sun Wu tradition or the Sun Bin tradition.

14. The relevant manuscripts have been translated by D. C. Lau and Roger T. Ames in their *Sun Bin: The Art of Warfare*. Among the thirty-one chapters of this corpus, the first fifteen, all of which include the quotational expression "Master Sun said/replied" and, in

some cases "King Wei asked" or "Tian Ji asked/said," may with reason be assigned to a putative *Sun Bin bingfa*. The remaining sixteen chapters, all of which lack these quotational expressions, should be relegated to the amorphous collection of military wisdom that was in circulation in the southern part of what is now Shandong Province during the second half of the second century B.C. The chapter entitled "Wu jiao fa" (The method of five types of training; number 15 in the translation of Lau and Ames) begins simply, "The Master said" (*zi yue*), and differs from the putative Sun Bin corpus both in terms of format and style. Consequently, it belongs with the loose collection of military chapters found at Yinque Shan, not with the alleged *Sun Bin bingfa* per se.

15. See n. 39.

16. The *Shi ji* was completed around 90 B.C. or slightly thereafter.

17. It is interesting to observe that Confucius himself had a military background. The legends concerning his father, Kong Shuliang He, in the *Zuo zhuan* (Chronicle of Zuo) place him in a decidedly military context, and the feudal class to which Confucius belonged was that of elite warriors (though they had fallen on hard times in Confucius' own day). There is also evidence to suggest for Confucius a hybrid ethnic profile (Eno 2003).

18. A series of reports on the finding and preliminary study of the Datong Han wooden strip manuscripts was published in *Wenwu* (Cultural relics) 2 (1981). Transcriptions of the relevant strips for the study of the *Sun Zi* have been republished in Xie and Liu (1993: 1:139–42) and in Huang (1996:257–63). Incidentally, it is purely coincidental that this group of Han manuscripts, a few of which are indirectly related to the *Sun Zi,* was unearthed at a site that goes by the modern name of Upper Sun Family Fortress. Shang Sunjia Zhai is located in the southeastern-most part of Datong County on the northern outskirts of Xining City. All together there are more than three hundred wooden strips from Shang Sunjia Zhai that are documents pertaining to military administration.

19. Sun Wú originally referred to two strategists, neither of whom was the shadowy author of *Sun Zi bingfa,* but to Sun Bin and Wú Qi (Petersen 1992b). When referring to the supposed author of the *Sun*

Zi, I shall usually omit the diacritic on the Wu of Sun Wu, except when necessary to contrast this name with the dyad "Sun Wú" (i.e., Sun Bin and Wú Qi).

20. It is misleading (and regrettable) when modern translators render "Sun Zi" as "Sun Wu" or "Sun Bin," as is frequently the case in various languages. The ambiguity of the original should be preserved, either simply as "Sun Zi" or as "Master Sun."

21. The Wu of this surname is written with yet another character. To distinguish this Wu from Wŭ and Wú, I leave it without a diacritic. The situation is further complicated by the fact that Wú Qi's surname is identical—both in character and in sound (including tone)—with the name of the southern state that Sun Wŭ was supposed to have served, viz., Wú.

22. The character used to write *xun* ("flee") has as its phonophore (sound-bearing element) the character for the surname Sun ("grandson"). The graph for *sun* ("grandson") is early, already appearing on the oracle bones around 1200 B.C. In contrast, the graph for *xun* ("flee") is much later, not occurring until about a millennium afterward. Hence, until the later invention of the specific graph for *xun*, which was formed by the addition of a radical indicating quick, yet intermittent and hesitant movement to the graph for *sun* (which—as noted above—served as the phonetic in the new graph for *xun*), the early graph (now pronounced *sun* in MSM) did double duty to write both the morpheme for "grandson" and for "flee." Indeed, at the time when the Sun Wu story was developing, it is altogether likely that his surname was actually meant to be read Xun (using MSM pronunciation), hence Xun Zi ("the Fugitive Master") or Xun Wu ("the Fugitive Warrior"), not Sun Zi or Sun Wu. See Wang Li 2000:215, 1450.

23. Wu and Chu were both southern states and shared a common border, whereas Qi was located far to the north and was separated from Wu by several intervening states.

24. Despite the fact that, already by the third c. B.C., the canonical *Sun Zi* had precipitated into the thirteen-chapter received text known to us today, scholars as late as the Tang period continued to be con-

fused by the ill-defined superabundance of Sun Zi writings that they believed (on the basis of various textual and bibliographical references) once existed. Thus Du Mu, in the preface to his commentary on the *Sun Zi* remarks, "The writings of Sun Wu amount to several hundred thousand words. Wei Wu (i.e., Cao Cao) pared their prolixity and penned their essence, completing this book." Du Mu is mistaken in thinking that it was Cao Cao who had reduced the *Sun Zi* to its canonical size, since archeological evidence from the second c. B.C. and textual evidence from the third c. B.C. alluded to above show that the work had already stabilized at thirteen chapters by that time. Furthermore, judging from an average chapter length of about 467 characters in the received text, if there really were a total of "several hundred thousand words" in the Sun Zi corpus writ large, that would mean there would once have been at least six or seven hundred chapters at one time, which is surely excessive. However, if we take all of the military treatises that were written during Han and earlier times, plus all of the recent manuscript finds of texts concerning military strategy and tactics, and look upon them as evolving from a prototypical Master Sun as the fountain of all wisdom about warfare, then Du Mu's overly generous estimate of the size of the Sun Zi corpus would begin to make some sense.

25. Since the kingdom of Wu is known to have conquered the capital of Chu, Ying, in the year 506 B.C., this date is seized upon by those who believe that Sun Wu was a real person as a solid datum upon which to hang the elaborate legend they have constructed for him. The problem with this is that there is no reliable pre-Han evidence for the existence of Sun Wu, much less for his participation in events that took place along the valley of the Yangtze River in the sixth c. B.C.

26. Sun Wu is also associated with Le'an in the *Yuanhe xingzuan* (Compilation of surnames from the primal accord reign period), compiled by Lin Bao in 812 A.D. (Lin 1994 [812]: vol. 1, s. 4, p. 461, entry 105). The entry simply declares (without proof) that some of Sun Wu's descendants lived at Le'an during the Han and later times. Unfortunately, both for the entry in the genealogical charts of the grand

councilors in the *Xin Tang shu* and the entry in the *Yuanhe xingzuan* that mention Sun Wu, it is impossible to bridge the gap of well over a thousand years from his alleged Spring and Autumn date. Furthermore, since there was no pre-Han place or governmental unit called Le'an, there is no way to connect the Le'an of these two Tang sources with a location of the Warring States or Spring and Autumn period. Finally, the Tang Le'an genealogy is itself contested by the fact that it can be identified either with modern Boxing County or with modern Huimin County in Shandong Province. Indeed, there are partisans for each of these counties as the birthplace of Sun Wu. Neither side has sufficient evidence to prove its case.

27. See Ye's *Xixue ji yan* (Recorded remarks on practice in learning), s. 46. The chief reason for Ye's suspicion of Sun Wu's historicity is that he was not mentioned in the *Zuo zhuan* (Chronicle of Zuo), the primary narrative (and I stress that word) for studying the history of the Spring and Autumn period. The final composition date of the *Zuo zhuan* is ca. 305 B.C. (Brooks 1994:49) Ye also believed that the type of warfare described in the *Sun Zi* was more characteristic of the Warring States period than of the Spring and Autumn period to which legend ascribes it.

Ye Shi was not alone in his skepticism about the *Sun Zi* as a product of the Spring and Autumn period. Chen Zhensun (fl. 1244, d. ca. 1262), in his *Zhi zhai shulu jieti* (Explanation of titles in the studio of straightness), commented: "Sun Wu [is said to have] served [King] Helu of Wu, but it is not mentioned in the *Zuo zhuan*. We really do not know what period he was from." During the Qing period (1616–1911), doubts concerning the historicity of Sun Wu and the *Sun Zi* intensified, but they have always been restricted to a small circle of critical scholars. For the general public (and even for uncritical scholars), Sun Wu was a real person who lived in the late sixth c. B.C. and who was the undisputed author of the *Sun Zi*.

Other skeptics have pointed out that the honorific, third-person "Master Sun said" formula at the beginning of each chapter clearly could not have been written by Sun Wu himself but must have been written by others about him. By themselves, the absence of Sun Wu (and the *Sun Zi,* for that matter) from the *Zuo zhuan* and the "Master Sun said" formula are not conclusive evidence against Sun Wu's existence during the Spring and Autumn period and his authorship of the *Sun Zi.* In the first place, the *Zuo zhuan* by no means mentions all the noteworthy figures of the Spring and Autumn period (e.g., various individuals in the *Analects*). In the second place, some books that are generally held to be composed of the words of the putative author (e.g., the *Wu Zi* [Sawyer 1993: 187–224, esp. 192]) do preface his quotations with such a formula.

In the final analysis, it is the incompatibility of the military methods and technologies described in the *Sun Zi* that disqualify it as a work of the Spring and Autumn period, and it is the internal stylistics plus the external lack of historical grounding that rule it out as the product of an individual named Sun Wu.

28. Whereas it is likely that the famous strategist named Sun Wu never lived, it is virtually certain that an actual person called Sun Bin (though that was not his real name) did exist. These probabilities concerning the historical veracity (or lack thereof) of Sun Wu and Sun Bin are mirrored in the nature of the texts attributed to them. Whereas the *Sun Zi* is a pastiche of apothegms loosely strung together, the *Sun Bin* consists of dialogs with historical personages, often embedded in a believable narrative context. The same is true of the *Wu Zi* and most other later military treatises.

29. In the narrowest, most specific sense, the word *bin* refers to removal of the kneecaps. More loosely, it could also signify various other degrees of mutilation or amputation of the toes, feet, or the whole of the lower leg.

30. E was located approximately fifteen miles northwest of modern Yanggu County in Shandong Province. Juan was about ten miles north of modern Juancheng, also in Shandong.

31. Tattoo is here referred to as a type of punishment, but less than a thousand years earlier, during the Shang Dynasty, it was a mark of prestige, as it was among the Thracians, the Scythians, and others in a wide belt across the Eurasian steppe, and as it still is among the Maori and other peoples who retain this old tradition.

32. Wei was often referred to as Liang after King Hui moved his capital from Anyi (about five miles northwest of modern Xiaxian, Shansi Province) to Da Liang (about five miles northwest of modern Kaifeng, Henan Province).

33. These are the operative terms of the first and third chapters of the *Sun Zi*.

34. The words translated here as "defenseless," "formations," and "power" are among the major concepts of the *Sun Zi*: *xu* ("empty, void"), *xing* ("form"), *shi* ("configuration").

35. There is still a city by this name in Hebei Province. It was the capital of the state of Zhao.

36. The location of this place is uncertain, but was probably in the province of Hebei or Shandong.

37. Sun Bin's old nemesis.

38. The Three Jin usually refers to the three states of Han, Zhao, and Wei that were created from the breakup of the Spring and Autumn state of Jin during the early years of the Warring States period. Here, however, Three Jin is a metonymy for the state of Wei.

39. The site of a celebrated battle that irrevocably altered the course of Warring States politics. It occurred in 341 B.C. and took place about thirty miles southeast of modern Daming, in Hebei Province.

40. Although this is one of the first recorded instances of the use of crossbows in battle, the fact that such a large number is mentioned indicates that it must not have been an entirely new weapon at this time.

41. By "the present generation" is meant the time of the writing of the *Shi ji*, i.e., the early first c. B.C. The translation follows closely that given in Nienhauser (1994:29–41) with minor changes, including the substitution of Hanyu Pinyin for Wade-Giles Romanization and the simplification or omission of most notes, which are many and detailed.

42. In the preceding pseudo-biography, Sun Wu is also referred to as Sun Zi ("Master Sun").

43. Aside from foregrounding Sun Wu with his own (albeit flimsy) biography in *Shi ji* 65 (translated in the appendix), Sima Qian also

mentions Sun Wu elsewhere in *Shi ji* (s. 25:1241; s. 31:1466 [ninth year of Helu]) as an outstanding military strategist who served Wu.

44. "Form" and "configuration" are technical terms in Chinese tactics, both receiving extensive discussion in the *Sun Zi*. See *xing* and *shi* in the section on "Key Terms" at the beginning of this volume.

45. The usual translation of *de* is "virtue," which in Modern English means primarily "moral excellence, goodness," then "chastity, especially of women," "efficacious or good quality," and finally "effective force or power" (*AH*, s.v.). The old, original meaning of "manly courage, valor" is now completely obsolete. Unfortunately, it is precisely the latter sense that is called for when interpreting most early occurrences of *de* that are not specifically concerned with Confucian ethics. Consequently, to bring out the sense required by the context here, I have used the Latin word *virtūs*, which conveys the correct connotation. Curiously, the order of the different senses of Latin *virtūs* is almost exactly the opposite of its English derivate, virtue: 1. the qualities typical of a true man, manly spirit, resolution, valor, steadfastness; 2. excellence of character or mind, worth, merit, ability; 3. moral excellence, virtue, goodness; 4. any attractive or valuable quality, potency, efficacy; 5. that in which something excels, special property (*Oxford Latin Dictionary*, 2073c–2074a). The main sense of the old Latin word still survives in the related English term "virile" (possessing or relating to the characteristics of an adult male; having or displaying masculine spirit, strength, vigor, power) and, oddly enough, in "virago" (essentially a "manly woman," with both negative and positive connotations: 1. noisy, scolding, domineering woman; 2. large, strong, courageous woman). The etyma of these words are *wer* in Old English and *vir* in Latin, both of which mean "man," and both of which go back to the Indo-European root *wi-ro* ("man"). There still exists in Modern English the adjective "doughty," which comes close to the range of meanings of Old Sinitic *de:* "able, capable, worthy, virtuous, valiant, brave, stout, formidable," but this word is now archaic and considered humorous, whereas the noun form which is called for, "doughtiness" ("valiantness, valor, stoutness"), has long been obsolete. If "doughty" and "doughtiness" were

still current in Modern English, they would make a good match for Old Sinitic *de*. For further discussion, see Mair (1990a:133–35).

46. In contrast to the three biographies of Sun Wu, Sun Bin, and Wu Qi that are squeezed into a single scroll (no. 65), and the first of which (Sun Wu's) gives every indication of having been completely concocted, Sima Qian affords an entire scroll to Wu Zixu's biography. It is interesting to note that Sima Qian even writes Sun Wu into Wu Zixu's biography by giving him a supporting role in determining when to attack Ying, the capital of Chu (Nienhauser 1994:53).

47. I have pointed out clear instances where "Sun Zi" signified the fictive Sun Wu and other equally unmistakable instances where "Sun Zi" signified Sun Bin.

48. Just as Sun Bin is far more a credible historical personage than is Sun Wu, so does Wu Qi come across as a largely believable individual who served as a general during the latter part of the rule of Marquis Wen (r. 445–396 B.C.) of Wei and, more importantly, during the reign of his son, Marquis Wu (r. 395–370 B.C.).

49. Presumably the *Sun Zi* and the *Wú Zi*, but we cannot say with absolute assurance that these abbreviated titles signify the *Sun Zi bingfa* attributed to Sun Wǔ and the *Wú Zi bingfa* attributed to Wú Qi (b. ca. 440–d. ca. 361 B.C.), since the *Sun Bin bingfa* could also have been called *Sun (Zi)*, while the *Sun Zi bingfa* itself was sometimes called the *Wu Sun Zi bingfa*.

50. In this chapter, Master Xun is referred to not by his real given name, Kuang, but as Qingzi, in reference to his official positions as Libationer and then Magistrate. Neither is he allowed to keep his own surname, but curiously is given the partially homophonous Sun, which is that of none other than the famous military strategists, Sun Bin and his imaginary ancestor, Sun Wu.

51. The surname of Master Xun (Xun Qing) is written with a totally different graph from that used to write the Xun meaning "flee" discussed in n. 22.

52. The word for "match," i.e., *di*, is the same word that also means "enemy." Hence, "nobody in the empire was a match/enemy for them."

53. The significance of the Iron Revolution for the military history of East Asia will be discussed in detail below under the rubric of "Techniques and Technology."

54. This would account for the more basic, elemental quality of the *Sun Zi* in comparison with the *Sun Bin,* which is more elaborate, more centered on the commanding general, and more attentive to actual formations.

55. Griffith (1963:6–11) offers numerous additional reasons why the *Sun Zi* could not have been written during the Spring and Autumn period, but must have been composed during Warring States times: the general term for metallic money, *jin,* is a Warring States phenomenon, yet it occurs five times in the *Sun Zi;* the word *zhu* with the meaning "sovereign, ruler" occurs eleven times in the *Sun Zi,* but during the Spring and Autumn period it meant "lord, master" (for addressing a minister); *shangjiang* ("commander of the upper/van army"), *zhongjiang* ("commander of the middle army"), and *xiajiang* ("commander of the lower/rear army") are Warring States terms, hence their occurrence in the *Sun Zi* disqualify it as a Spring and Autumn work; specific terms for chamberlain or receptionist (*yezhe*), retainers or bodyguards (*sheren*) that occur in the *Sun Zi* were not in circulation during the Spring and Autumn period but were common during the Warring States. The cosmological notion of "five phases" or "five elements" (*wuxing*) that are in constant mutation did not develop until the Warring States, yet they occur in *Sun Zi* 6. All of these anachronisms provide internal evidence from the *Sun Zi* itself that the text was written during the fourth c., not at the end of the sixth c. as traditionally believed.

56. These dates have been extracted from the review article of E. Bruce Brooks (1994), pp. 59–62, which are a densely argued brief for the *Sun Zi* as an accretional text, describing its growth—in an interstate context—during the period from ca. 345 B.C. to ca. 272 B.C. Brooks (1994) is essential reading for anyone who wishes to understand the intellectual and historical setting in which the *Sun Zi* developed. Working together with A. Taeko Brooks, he employs accretional

theory to show that nearly all pre-Han Sinitic texts were built up over a period of time and reveal traces of the intellectual and political debates that stimulated their composition. The Brookses have applied this analytical technique in its fullest form and to greatest effect in a revolutionary work entitled *The Original Analects: Sayings of Confucius and His Successors* (1998). The Brookses employ a large battery of tools in their investigations of texts such as the *Sun Zi*, including linguistics, stylistics, and text criticism. While critics of the Brookses' studies complain that their findings are overly precise, few would now doubt that their basic methodology has tremendous heuristic value and that it has transformed historical research on early Sinitic texts. As for the specific dates proposed for the individual chapters of the *Sun Zi*, we do not need to accept them as utterly exact and engraved in stone. Indeed, the Brookses themselves have continued diligently to refine their analyses of the entire corpus of Han and earlier texts, so they would undoubtedly now make some small adjustments in the dates given here for the chapters of the *Sun Zi*. None of this, however, should negate the fundamental discovery that the *Sun Zi* developed over a period of time lasting from around the middle of the fourth century B.C. to the beginning of the second quarter of the third century B.C.

57. The social, institutional, and historical background of the rise of mass infantry armies during the fourth and third centuries is studied in Mark Edward Lewis' *Sanctioned Violence in Early China* (1990).

58. Economic matters per se are dealt with more overtly in chapter 2, which was probably written a couple of years before chapter 1, the penultimate chapter chronologically.

59. It is reassuring that Lewis (2005:5) independently arrived at the conclusion that the last chapter of the *Sun Zi* must have been written after 284 B.C., and he did so by completely different means than Brooks. Lewis also agrees with Brooks that the earlier chapters of the book were begun around the middle of the fourth century.

60. The total number of characters in the *Sun Zi* and the proportion of *gu* among them will vary slightly from edition to edition. For my computations, I have relied on the variorum edition in Lau (1992),

since it is based on careful collation of the best available texts and provides valuable frequency charts in an appendix (the source of all the figures for the four military texts analyzed in this section).

61. Not all of the instances of *gu* in the texts analyzed here are illative conjunctions, but the total occurrences of this character are meaningful for my analysis, inasmuch as illatives constitute over 90 percent (95 occurrences) of all instances of *gu* in the *Sun Zi*.

62. The high frequency of *gu* in the *Sun Zi* and in the *Dao de jing* contrasts not only with the lower frequency for *gu* in the three other military texts analyzed above, but also with the frequency of *gu* in a wide range of classical and medieval texts written in Literary Sinitic. Out of a total of 2,555 different characters in nineteen concordances, *gu* is placed in a group of five characters that ranked twenty-sixth in terms of frequency of occurrence (Brooks and Brooks 1976: esp. p. 8).

63. By "illatives," I mean illative coordinating conjunctions such as "for, hence, so, thus, therefore, as a consequence, as a result, for this reason, so that, so then."

64. By "true illatives," I mean that B really does follow logically and/or sequentially from A in the statement "A therefore B." By "false illative," I mean that B does not logically or sequentially follow from A in the statement "A therefore B."

65. Similar analyses could be performed for the prominence of sentence-final *ye* serving as a definitional particle as well as for other rhetorical features of the text, but that will have to wait for more specialized linguistic studies.

66. The general west → east cultural gradient shifted in the opposite direction during the Middle Ages, when the Huns, Mongols, and other fighting hordes from the eastern half of Asia scourged western Eurasia for centuries.

67. Still the most profound book-length study of early bronze weapons in the EAH is Max Loehr's *Chinese Bronze Age Weapons*. In it, while sensitive to distinctive differences, the author points out numerous parallels and analogies between the shapes and ornamentation of ancient Chinese weapons and those of Central Siberia, Iran (Persia,

Luristan), the Caucasus, and Mesopotamia (Sumeria), as well as Hallstatt (in what is now Austria). His detailed comparisons between Shang and Zhou weapons, on the one hand, and Siberian artifacts (from Minusinsk, Krasnoyarsk, and Karasuk) belonging to the Afanasievo and Andronovo cultures are particularly revealing. Loehr stresses, in particular, the Iranian influence that passed through Western Central Asia and South Siberia, then farther east between the Altai and Tängri Tagh (Tian Shan; Heavenly Mountains) to the Gansu Corridor and the Ordos (Mair 2005a).

68. See n. 79 for the date and origin of the crossbow.

69. In attempting to establish a relative chronology for the early military treatises, it should be noted that cavalry forces are mentioned twelve times in the *Wu Zi,* but not once in the *Sun Zi,* the *Wei Liao Zi,* and the *Sima fa.* This would seem to indicate fairly clearly that the *Wu Zi* was compiled in the third c. B.C. or later, while the other three texts were probably put together mainly before the end of the fourth c. B.C. For an English translation of the passage from Du You's *Tong dian* that discusses the ten advantages of using cavalry, see Lau and Ames (2003:179).

70. One wonders whether the *Sun Zi* really is a southern work. Perhaps the alleged association of the putative author with the southern figures King Helu (or Helü) and Wu Zixu is yet another component of the overall simulacrum that envelops the *Sun Zi.* According to the Brookses, the *Sun Zi* is a work of the state of Lu, or perhaps the state of Qi, both of which were in the north (the modern province of Shandong) (1998:7).

71. More than half a dozen different sets of dates have been proposed by various scholars for the lifespan of Mo Zi. Despite the disparity, there is a general consensus that he was born around the time of the death of Confucius (550–479 B.C.) and that he died around the time Mencius (382–279 B.C.) was born.

72. Specialists on the *Mo Zi* maintain that none of its chapters date from the time of the master himself but that the entire work was put together by several generations of his followers during a period stretching from around the beginning of the fourth century to the

latter half of the second century B.C. The military chapters are generally considered to be the latest of the entire Mician corpus, extending from approximately 375 to 225 B.C., with the technical chapters on tunneling (62), swarming (63), and walls and gates (52) being the latest among the military chapters, ranging from roughly the beginning of the third century to the last quarter of the same century (Graham 1993; Brooks and Brooks 1998:5, 258–62; Yates 1980; Needham and Yates 1994; Johnston 2007). Of the twenty military chapters that were originally part of the *Mo Zi*, only eleven are now extant.

73. This is not to imply that the Greco-Roman corpus of military treatises is impoverished. The bibliography of Mayor (2003) lists fifty-one Greek and Latin authors who discuss military matters.

74. I shall refer to him by the Greek form of his name, instead of the Latinate form, Aeneas, which is often used by modern writers.

75. Aineias attributes the invention of this clever technique to "the distant past . . . when Amasis attempted tunnelling during his siege of Barka." Whereas the Barkaians and later Greeks employed a bronze shield-plate to detect and amplify the sounds of digging beneath the surface of the ground, the *Mo Zi* (chap. 62) specifies the use of large earthen pots called *ying* as geophones.

76. In the surviving portions of Aineias' text, he mentions the use of vinegar only as a flame retardant (92), but other Greek and Roman authors were quite familiar with its efficacy as an antidote for irritating substances released by the enemy, which is exactly the reason why the *Mo Zi* (end of chap. 62) enjoins the storing up of large quantities of vinegar in basins that were to be distributed in the defenders' tunnels. This practical lesson of the ancients has not been lost on modern demonstrators who face tear gas wearing handkerchiefs that have been moistened with vinegar (Mayor 2003:221–22).

77. Aineias 8.1 mentions another book of his called *Preparations,* which amounts to an exact equivalent of the *bei* chapters in the *Mo Zi*. In 14.2 he further notes yet another of his works, entitled *Procurement,* which mirrors concerns expressed in some of the first few chapters of the *Sun Zi,* and in 21.2 he refers to still another work that is now

lost, *Encampment,* which would have engaged topics taken up in the middle chapters of the *Sun Zi.*

78. The *Mo Zi* as a whole is so much concerned with science (e.g., optics) and engineering (e.g., defensive machinery) that one suspects Mo Zi and his school to have been technocrats. Indeed, his surname Mo ("[black] ink") has been speculatively explained as deriving from the use of this dark substance with a carpenter's string to mark a straight line.

79. The earliest known crossbows in the world appear to have been created about 2,400 years ago by Austroasiatic peoples in Southeast Asia, and perhaps ultimately by the Mon branch of Austroasiatics in South Asia (Norman and Mei 1976:293–95). The bellows were most likely devised in association with ironworking, perhaps in the Black Sea area where ferrous metallurgy first developed about 3,300 years ago, although the first-known textual reference to bellows in the world may be that in the *Mo Zi.* In *Zhuang Zi,* chapters 12 (*gao*) and 14 (*jiegao*), especially the former, the well-sweep is derided as being an overly clever contraption. Reading these passages, which were probably written between about 300 and 250 B.C., almost makes one feel that the well-sweep is looked upon as an alien importation. Indeed, it is probably nothing more than a shadoof (or shaduf), which has a long history in Egypt and India. One of the uses of the well-sweep in the *Mo Zi* was to work large bellows at the base of the city wall that were intended to pump smoke into the tunnels dug by the enemy.

80. Innovations even in the more esoteric aspects of warfare (e.g., similar incendiary and poisonous weapons, animals as delivery vehicles for such weapons, comparable or identical combustible mixtures and projectile systems) were developing at roughly the same period across Eurasia, with South Asia and East Asia in general lagging a century or more behind the West in these developments, and Central Asia falling roughly in the middle timewise, just as it is geographically situated in the center. Although the terrifying Greek Fire is usually associated with the Byzantine Greeks of medieval times, it was already in use by around 430–434 B.C. (Mayor 2003:11ff [time

line], see also 202 ff and passim; Partington 1960:28, and esp. ch. 6 [237–97, "Pyrotechnics and Firearms in China"]; Sawyer 2004:115 ff).

Carman (2004 [1955]:1) recounts a memorable early instance of fire being conveyed by animals, when Samson tied firebrands to the tails of foxes and sent them against the Philistines. Tian Dan of the state of Qi did the same thing with cattle about a thousand years later toward the end of the Warring States period. And Kauṭilya—probably around a century before Tian Dan's time—advocated attaching incendiary powders to birds, cats, mongooses, and monkeys (Sawyer 2004:117; Mayor 2003:203).

81. The name is also interpreted as referring to economics or statecraft.

82. Modern, critical scholarship dates various parts of the *Arthaśāstra* to the period from ca. 290 B.C. to 300 A.D. and consequently asserts that Kauṭilya could not have written the entire book. Nonetheless, Kangle (1988 [1965–69]:59–115) gives abundant evidence supporting the view that Kauṭilya initiated the writing of the book and that he was responsible for the bulk of it. A large part of the doubt over the early dating of the *Arthaśāstra* is due to statistical analysis of its vocabulary as displaying elements that could not have been present at the time of Kauṭilya, but this could be the result of editorial tampering during the preparation of later recensions.

83. The famous dictum of *Sun Zi* 1, "Warfare is a way of deception," is echoed by the very name of Kauṭilya, which is commonly said to be derived from *kuṭila* ("crooked, dishonest, deceitful"). Thus Kauṭilya was simply "Mr. Devious," which Master Sun would have applauded. In actuality, such an explanation of the name can only be arrived at punningly, since most authorities view it as the author's Brahmanical *gotra* ("cowshed," i.e., exogamous patrilineal sibship) name. Another cognomen for Kauṭilya was Cāṇakya ("made of chick peas"), which makes him sound rather innocuous and a disappointment to all good Machiavellians. However, he was also called Viṣṇugupta ("hidden by Viṣṇu"), which restores a bit of the mystery to the man (although some scholars think that the latter name may refer to a different person, who, they believe, had a hand in writing the *Arthaśāstra*).

84. For annotated bibliographical descriptions of these two works, see the articles by Hans-Hermann Schmidt in Schipper and Verellen (2004: vol. 1, pp. 69–70, and vol. 2, p. 690).

85. The unstable nature of the Guodian bamboo-strip *Dao de jing* qua written text can be seen, among other things, by the fact that the most important concept in it, namely Tao (the Way), is written with two totally different graphs in the same bundle (A) of strips. These are: 1. the usual character written with a "head" (*shou*) to the right and above radical no. 162 (*chuo* ["go step by step"]), and 2. a rare, archaic variant (now usually read *hang*) that consists of "man" (*ren* [radical no. 9]) sandwiched between the two components of radical no. 144 (*xing* ["walk"]).

86. Though the term *wuwei* itself does not occur in the *Sun Zi,* its ethos is plentifully evident throughout the text.

87. In pointing out the Taoistic affinities and associations of the *Sun Zi,* I by no means wish to identify it as belonging to the Taoist school of thought per se. It is "clearly the work of practical military men concerned primarily with matters of tactics and strategy, and it is difficult to associate [it] with any particular philosophical school" (Rickett 1985:267).

88. See n. 6 above.

89. There are many conflicting opinions about when the Tangut state was founded, with some holding that it began in 1032 or even as early as ca. 982. The complicated Sinoform Tangut script was based upon, but totally different from, Chinese characters and is still largely undeciphered (Sofronov 1991; Zhou Youguang 1991).

90. A facsimile of the Tangut translation may be found in Keping (1979:477–578), also in Xie and Liu (1993:1:691–792).

91. For a complete transcription of the Manchu text, together with word-for-word English glosses, see the author's online publication entitled "*Soldierly Methods*: Introduction and Notes for an Iconoclastic Translation of *Sun Zi bingfa*" in *Sino-Platonic Papers.*

The Manchus were a nation of great warriors who ably ruled the East Asian Heartland for nearly three centuries and extended its borders to hitherto unimagined regions, many of which are still attached to the People's Republic of China. They were the founders of the Qing ("Pure") (1644–1911), one of the longest and most glorious dynasties in Chinese history, albeit the last.

The Manchu translation of the *Sun Zi* is attributed to Qiying (Kiying; 1790–1858), a high-ranking imperial clansman. For a fascinating account of Qiying's eventful life, particularly in dealing with foreign powers during the period of the Opium Wars (mid-nineteenth c.), see Fang Chao-ying's detailed article in Hummel (1943:1:130b–134b).

92. In an effort to determine whether there is any scrap of evidence in support of the contention that Napoleon was familiar with the *Sun Zi*, I read through sixty-five biographies and studies of Napoleonic history but could not find a single reference to the *Sun Zi*. Unless someone can produce solid evidence that Napoleon was aware of the *Sun Zi*, I believe that we should declare the rumor to be false and dead.

93. See chap. 3 n. 10.

CHAPTER 1

(Initial) Assessments[1]

The opening chapter emphasizes the importance of evaluation and planning prior to battle. In so doing, it examines the fundamental criteria for determining victory or defeat. Also stressed at the outset is the need to attack the enemy when he is least prepared and to do what he least expects.

Master Sun said,[2]

> Warfare[3] is a great affair of the state.[4]
>> The field of life and death,
>> The way of preservation and extinction.
> It cannot be left unexamined.[5]

Therefore,
>> Measure it in terms of five factors,
>> Weigh it by means of seven assessments,[6]
>>> and seek out its circumstances.

The first factor is the Way,[7]
The second is Heaven,[8]
The third is Earth,[9]
The fourth is Generalship,
The fifth is Method.

The Way is that which causes the people to be of the same mind with their superior.[10]
Therefore,
They are committed to die with him,
They are committed to live with him,
and not fear danger.[11]

Heaven comprises yin and yang,[12] cold and heat,[13] the ordering of time.[14]

Earth comprises distant or near, precipitous or gentle, broad or narrow,[15] positions conducive to death or life.[16]

Generalship comprises knowledge, trustworthiness, humaneness, bravery, and sternness.

Method comprises organization of units, official channels, and control of matériel.

The general must be informed about all five of these factors, but only he who truly understands them will be victorious, while those who fail to understand them will be defeated. Therefore, when weighing warfare by means of seven assessments and seeking out its circumstances, one should ask:

Which side's ruler possesses the Way?
Which side's general is more capable?
Which side possesses the advantages of Heaven and
    Earth?

Which side exercises its rules and methods more
rigorously?
Which side has the stronger army?
Which side has officers and troops that are more highly
trained?
Which side is more transparent in dispensing rewards
and punishments?

Through these considerations, I can foretell victory or defeat.

If you[17] will heed my assessments and act on them, you will certainly be victorious, and I shall remain here; if you will not heed
my assessments and act on them, you will certainly be defeated,
and I shall leave.[18]

When an advantageous assessment has been heeded, one must
create for it a favorable configuration to assist the war effort exter-
nally.[19] A favorable configuration is one that signifies the creation
of power[20] in accordance with advantage.

Warfare is[21] a way of deception.[22]

Therefore,
When one is capable, give the appearance of[23] being
incapable.
When one is active, give the appearance of being inactive.
When one is near, give the appearance of being far.
When one is far, give the appearance of being near.

When one's opponents are greedy for advantage, tempt
   them.
When one's opponents are in chaos, seize them.
When one's opponents are secure, prepare for them.
When one's opponents are strong, evade them.
When one's opponents are angry, aggravate them.
When one's opponents are humble, make them
   arrogant.
When one's opponents are at ease, make them weary.
When one's opponents are friendly to each other, divide
   them.

Attack them when they are unprepared;
Come forth when they are not expecting you to do so.[24]

Herein lies the victoriousness of the strategist, which cannot be
divulged beforehand.

Now, he who is victorious in the temple computations[25] before
battle is the one who receives more counting rods. He who is not
victorious in the temple computations before battle is the one who
receives fewer counting rods. The one with more counting rods
wins,[26] and the one with fewer counting rods loses. How much less
chance of winning is there for someone who receives no counting
rods at all!
   Through our observation of these calculations, victory and defeat are apparent.

CHAPTER 2

Doing Battle

This chapter focuses on the importance of human, material, and financial resources for war making. It puts a premium on quick victory and is opposed to prolonged war. This stands in sharp contrast to Mao Zedong's advocacy of long, drawn-out war for wearing down a stronger enemy while building up one's own forces.

Master Sun said,

The method of waging war invariably requires
a thousand swift chariots,
a thousand heavy carts,
a hundred thousand armored troops,
and the transportation of grain over a thousand tricents.

Then there are
internal and external expenditures,
provisions for missions sent to and fro,

the raw material for glue and lacquer,[1]
the supplying of equipment,
which amounts to a thousand pieces of gold per day.

Only after that can an army of a hundred thousand men be mobilized.

The purpose of engaging in battle is to win.[2] A prolonged war wears down the soldiers and dampens their ardor. If they are made to attack cities, their strength will be exhausted. If the army is exposed in the field for long, the kingdom's resources will be inadequate. If the soldiers' strength is exhausted and goods are depleted, the feudal lords will take advantage of the weakness and rise up. If this happens, even an intelligent commander will not be able to remedy the results.

Therefore,

in war, I have only heard that even the dull-witted commander strives for a quick victory, but have never seen a clever general aim for a prolonged engagement. There has never been a case of prolonged war from which a kingdom benefited.

Therefore,

he who does not thoroughly understand the harm of waging war cannot thoroughly understand the advantages of waging war.

He who is skilled at waging war
        never permits a second conscription per campaign,
        never permits a third transportation of supplies,
        procures provisions from his own country,
        relies for grain on the enemy.

Therefore,
> foodstuffs for the army will be sufficient.

A kingdom is impoverished by having to supply an army at a distance; when the army is supplied at a distance, the common people are impoverished.[3] Whoever is close to an army experiences inflation; wherever there is inflation, the economy of the common people suffers. When the economy suffers, the community is beset by local levies.

The exhaustion of the troops' strength and the depletion of resources lead to emptiness within the households of the Central Plains.[4] Seven-tenths of the common people's expenditures are consumed by the war effort; six-tenths of the public expenditures are consumed on account of ruined chariots, wearied horses, armor, helmets, arrows, crossbows, halberds, shields, pavises, bullocks, and carts.

Therefore,
> the wise general strives to eat the enemy's food. Eating one bushel of the enemy's grain is equal to bringing twenty bushels of our own. A picul[5] of the enemy's fodder is equal to twenty of our own.

Therefore,
> if one wants the soldiers to kill the enemy, one must enrage them; if one wants the soldiers to derive profit from the enemy, one must induce them with goods.[6]

Therefore,
> in chariot warfare where more than ten of the enemy's chariots are captured, one should reward whoever made the first capture.

Those who change the flags and banners of the enemy chariots should be allowed to mix them in with our own and mount them. Likewise, troops who come over to our side should be treated well and taken care of. This is called "becoming stronger through vanquishing the enemy."[7]

Therefore,
> in war, swift victory is valued,[8]
> prolongation is devalued.

Therefore,
> the general who understands warfare is
>> the arbiter of fate for the people,
>> the guarantor of security for the nation.

CHAPTER 3

Planning for the Attack

*The main point of this chapter is that one should only go into battle when
one has the advantage. It closes with the famous dictum about knowing
oneself and one's opponent.*

Master Sun said,

The method of waging war holds that it is always best

> to take[1] the opposing country intact,[2]
> whereas destroying the opposing country is next best.
>
> Taking an opposing army intact is best,
> whereas destroying it is next best.
>
> Taking an opposing regiment intact is best,
> whereas destroying it is next best.

Taking an opposing company intact is best,
whereas destroying it is next best.

Taking an opposing squad[3] intact is best,
whereas destroying it is next best.

For this reason,
being victorious a hundred times in a hundred battles is not
the most excellent approach. Causing the enemy forces to submit
without a battle is the most excellent approach.[4]

Therefore,
the most superior stratagem in warfare is to stymie the
enemy's plans;
the next best is to stymie his alliances;
the next best is to stymie his troops;
the worst is to attack his walled cities

The method of attacking walled cities should be resorted to only
when there is no other option.

To attack a walled city, it is necessary to construct mantlets and
assault wagons,[5] and to make ready siege machines, which require
three months to complete; then mounds of earth must be piled up
against the walls, again requiring three months to finish. Unable to
overcome his anger, the general sends his troops to clamber up the
walls like ants. A third of his troops are killed, and still the city does
not fall. This is the disaster that results from attacking walled cities.[6]

Therefore,
he who is skilled at waging war causes his opponent's soldiers to
submit without having to fight a battle, causes his opponent's cities

to fall without having to attack them, and destroys his opponent's kingdom without having to engage in prolonged war. Instead, with a comprehensive strategy, he contends before all under heaven. Therefore,

> his soldiers are not worn down, yet his advantages are preserved intact. This is the method of attack by stratagem.[7]

Therefore,

> the method of waging war is
>> to encircle the enemy when one has ten times the
>>> number of his forces,
>> to attack the enemy when one has five times the number
>>> of his forces,
>> to divide the enemy when one has twice the number of
>>> his forces,
>> to battle the enemy when one's forces are equal to his.[8]

Therefore,

> he who stubbornly persists though his forces are fewer
> will be captured by an enemy whose forces are more
>> numerous.

Now, the general is the buttress of the kingdom. When the buttress is solid, the kingdom will surely be strong; when the buttress is defective, the kingdom will surely be weak.

Therefore,

> there are three respects in which the army may be troubled by the ruler. When the ruler does not understand that the army cannot advance, yet he orders it to advance, or when the ruler does

not understand that the army cannot retreat, yet he orders it to retreat, this is called "hobbling the army."

When the ruler does not understand the affairs of the triple army,[9] yet participates in its administration, the officers and troops will be confused. When the ruler does not understand the expediency of the triple army, yet participates in its supervision, the officers and troops will be suspicious. When the triple army is both confused and suspicious, difficulties from the feudal lords will have arrived. This is called bringing chaos to one's own army and inviting the victory of one's opponents.

Therefore,

there are five respects in which one may have foreknowledge of victory. He who knows when one can do battle and when one cannot do battle will be victorious. He who recognizes the functionality of the many and the few will be victorious. He who can cause superiors and inferiors to share the same desires will be victorious. He who is prepared and lies in wait for one who is unprepared will be victorious. The general who is capable and whose ruler does not interfere will be victorious. These five respects are the way to foreknowledge of victory.

Therefore,

it is said, "He who knows his opponent and knows himself will not be imperiled in a hundred battles. He who knows not his opponent but knows himself will win one and lose one. He who knows neither his opponent nor himself will surely be imperiled in every battle."[10]

CHAPTER 4

Positioning

The chief tenet of this chapter is that it is necessary to place one's army in an unassailable position, then to seek out weaknesses in the enemy's deployment that can be exploited. To strike at the enemy from a vantage of overwhelming superiority is the aim of the capable commander.

Master Sun said,

Those in the past who were skilled in battle first made themselves invincible so as to confront the vincibility of the enemy. Invincibility depends upon oneself; vincibility depends upon the enemy.

Therefore,
he who is skilled in battle can make himself invincible, but cannot cause the enemy to be vincible.

Therefore,
it is said, "Victory can be foretold, but cannot be forced."

When the enemy is invincible, we should adopt a defensive posture; when the enemy is vincible, we should launch an attack.[1] We adopt a defensive posture when our resources are insufficient; we launch an attack when our resources are abundant.[2] He who is skilled at adopting a defensive posture will hide away beneath the deepest level of earth; he who is skilled at launching an attack will take action to the highest level of heaven.

Therefore,
he can protect himself and achieve total victory.

Foreseeing victory does not exceed that which may be known to the masses of men; it is not the most excellent approach.[3] Being victorious in battle and having all under heaven[4] acknowledge one's skill is not the most excellent approach.

Therefore,
lifting up a strand of fine animal hair newly grown in autumn[5] does not require great strength; seeing the sun and the moon does not require keen eyesight; hearing thunder does not require a sensitive ear. Those in antiquity who were said to be skilled in battle won their victories against those who were easy to vanquish.

Therefore,
the victories of one who is skilled in battle do not evince a reputation for wisdom and do not bespeak brave merit.[6]

Therefore,
that he will be victorious in battle is not in doubt, and the reason it is not in doubt is because the arrangements he makes necessarily lead to victory; that is to say, he is victorious over an opponent who has already been placed in a situation that leads to defeat.

Therefore,
> he who is skilled in battle establishes himself in an undefeatable position, and does not let slip the inevitable defeat of his enemy.

For this reason,
> being victorious in war depends upon first preparing the conditions for victory and then seeking battle with the enemy;[7] being defeated in war results from first engaging in battle and then seeking victory. He who is skilled at waging war cultivates the way[8] and protects the law.

Therefore,
> he can serve as the governor of victory and defeat.

The method of war: first is measuring,[9] second is estimating,[10] third is counting,[11] fourth is comparing,[12] fifth is gauging.[13] The actual conditions of the battleground give rise to measuring, measuring gives rise to estimating, estimating gives rise to counting, counting gives rise to comparing, and comparing gives rise to gauging.

Therefore,
> the victor in war vis-à-vis the vanquished is like comparing a hundredweight to an ounce; the vanquished in war vis-à-vis the victor is like comparing an ounce to a hundredweight.[14] The victor directing his men in battle is like releasing a thousand fathoms[15] of water that have been dammed up in a chasm. It is all a matter of positioning.[16]

CHAPTER 5

Configuration[1]

In this chapter, the focus is on the general's ability to command his army, maximizing its potential through conventional and unconventional tactics. Although discussed only in one relatively brief section of this chapter, the interplay of conventional and unconventional is one of the key tactical concepts introduced in the Sun Zi.

Master Sun said,

Managing masses of troops is similar to managing a small group of soldiers; it is a question of division and enumeration.[2] Sending masses of troops into combat is similar to sending small groups of soldiers into combat; it is a question of forms and terms.[3] The masses of the triple army may be caused to have an encounter with the enemy and yet not be defeated; it is a question of conventional and unconventional tactics.[4] The application of military force should be like throwing a grindstone on an egg: it is a question of emptiness and solidity.

It is common to join battle with conventional tactics and to achieve victory through unconventional tactics.

Therefore,

he who is good at devising unconventional tactics has a repertoire that is as unlimited as heaven and earth, as inexhaustible as the rivers and streams. It may seem that his unconventional tactics have come to an end, but then they begin all over again like the waxing and waning of the sun and moon; they may seem to have died, but then they are reborn like the cycle of the four seasons. There are only five notes,[5] yet the transformations of these five notes afford infinite aural pleasure. There are only five colors,[6] yet the transformations of these five colors afford infinite visual pleasure. There are only five flavors, yet the transformations of these five flavors afford infinite gustatory pleasure.[7] The basic battle configurations are only the conventional and the unconventional, yet the transformations of these two types of tactics afford infinite possibilities. The conventional and the unconventional give rise to each other, like a circle that has neither beginning nor end. Who could ever exhaust their potential?

The swiftness of a raging torrent can sweep away boulders; this is due to its configurative momentum. The swiftness of a diving raptor can tear its prey apart; this is due to its instinctive timing.

For this reason,

he who is skilled in battle builds up an overpowering configuration that he [releases] with instantaneous timing. The configuration that he constructs is like a fully drawn and cocked crossbow;[8] the timing of his release is like pulling its trigger.

Amidst the fluttering of flags and banners and the jostling of men and horses, the general cannot permit chaos to sweep through his army even in the chaos of combat. In the confused murk of swirling forces, the commander must keep his formation intact so that he cannot be defeated. Chaos may arise out of order; cowardice may be born from bravery; weakness may come from strength. Bringing order out of chaos depends upon enumeration;[9] eliciting bravery from cowardice depends upon configuration; developing strength from weakness depends upon formation.

Therefore,

he who is skilled at manipulating the enemy presents him with a shifting variety of formations[10] to which he must respond, and he entices the enemy with hollow gains that he will surely snatch. The capable general manipulates the enemy with empty advantages, while his main force lies in wait.[11]

Therefore,

he who is skilled in battle places emphasis upon configuration and does not put undue responsibilities on his subordinates.

Therefore,

he can select suitable subordinates and take advantage of configuration. When he who takes advantage of configuration sends his subordinates into battle, it is like turning over a log or a boulder. The nature of wood and stone is such that when they are stable they are still, but when they are precarious they move; when they are square they stop, but when they are round they roll.

Therefore,

the configuration of one who is skilled at sending his subordinates into battle is like turning over a round boulder at the top of a mountain ten thousand feet high; it is all a matter of configuration.[12]

CHAPTER 6

Emptiness and Solidity

This is the third longest chapter in the book, but it only touches upon the subject of the title in the last, short section, another indication that the Sun Zi is chiefly a compilation of military lore and not the composition of a single author ab novo. Most of the chapter is taken up with an extended discussion of the need to manipulate one's enemy and to avoid being manipulated by him. Also touched upon is the wisdom of adroit response, together with subtle variations on the theme of chapter 4, xing ("form, shape, position").

Master Sun said,

Whoever occupies the battleground first and awaits the enemy is relaxed, while the one who arrives at the battleground later and rushes into battle is fatigued.

Therefore,

he who is skilled in battle controls the movements of others but does not allow his own movements to be controlled by others. The ability to cause the enemy to come of his own accord is the result of enticing him with advantage; the ability to cause the enemy not to come is the result of dissuading him with disadvantage.[1]

Therefore,
     if the enemy is relaxed, one may make him fatigued; if he is full, one may make him hungry; if he is settled, one may make him move.

Appear where the enemy cannot rush to;[2] rush to where he does not expect you. The army that marches a thousand tricents without becoming fatigued marches to where the foe is not entrenched. The army that is sure to take the object it attacks, attacks where the foe does not defend; the army that holds firm when it defends, defends where the foe does not attack.

Therefore,
     he who is skilled at attacking causes the enemy not to know where to defend; he who is skilled at defending causes the enemy not to know where to attack.

     Mysterious! So mysterious is he that he has no shape. Daemonic! So daemonic is he that he makes no sound.

Therefore,
     he can determine the fate of the enemy.

He who advances but cannot be resisted charges toward the empty spots in the enemy's defenses. He who retreats but cannot be pursued withdraws so rapidly that the enemy cannot catch up with him.

Therefore,

if I wish to do battle, even though the enemy is within a high fortress encircled by a deep moat, he cannot but do battle with me because I attack where he must come to the rescue. If I do not wish to do battle, though I do no more than draw a line on the ground and defend behind it, the enemy cannot do battle with me because I have taken a position contrary to where he wishes to go.

Therefore,

I cause my enemy to reveal his dispositions while hiding my own. Thus, my forces are intact while those of my enemy are divided. My forces are intact, a single whole, whereas my enemy's forces are divided into ten parts, so that I have ten times his strength when I attack one portion of his forces. Thus my forces are numerous while the enemy's forces are few. Being able to strike his few forces with my numerous forces imposes constraints upon those who would engage in battle with me.

The places where I might engage the enemy in battle cannot be known by him. Since he cannot know where I might engage him, the places where he must be prepared for me are many. Since the places where the enemy must be prepared for me are many, there are few places where he will be ready to engage in battle with me.

Therefore,

if he prepares for me in front, he will have few forces in the rear; if he prepares for me in the rear, he will have few forces in front. If he prepares for me on the left, he will have few forces on the right. If he prepares for me on the right, he will have few forces on the left. If he prepares for me everywhere, then his forces will be few everywhere. Fewness results from having to prepare for your opponent wherever he wants you to; numerousness results from causing your opponent to prepare for you wherever you want him to.

Therefore,

if one can foreknow the place of battle and can foreknow the time of battle, one can join in battle even though it be a thousand tricents away. If one cannot foreknow the place of battle and cannot foreknow the time of battle, one's left side will not be able to rescue one's right side, one's right side will not be able to rescue one's left side, one's front will not be able to rescue one's rear, and one's rear will not be able to rescue one's front. How much less will one be able to do so at a distance of several tens of tricents or even nearer by several tricents away?

By my considerations, although the people of Yue[3] have many soldiers, of what benefit are they in determining victory or defeat?

Therefore,

it is said: "Victory is something that can be created."[4] Although the enemy's forces may be numerous, I can cause him to be unable to fight me with all of them at the same time and in the same place.[5]

Therefore,

I analyze my foe to know the strengths and weaknesses of his plans; I agitate my foe to know the stability of his principles; I show him just enough of my positions that I may know whether he is in a desperate situation; I probe him so that I may know where he has a surplus and where he has a deficiency.

Therefore,

the extreme skill in showing one's positions may reach to the degree of there seeming to be no position. When there are no positions, even deeply planted spies cannot detect them, and even a wise foe will not be able to make plans against me. Though victory based on my positions may be displayed before the masses, the masses cannot know them. The people may all know the positions whereby I achieve victory, but no one knows how I utilize those positions to produce victory.

Therefore,

I never repeat the means whereby I achieve victory, but responsively adjust my positions with infinitude.

The form of a body of soldiers resembles that of water. Water's natural form is such that it avoids heights and rushes toward depths. The natural form of a body of soldiers is such that it avoids solidity and strikes at emptiness.[6] Water produces currents in accordance with the terrain; soldiers produce victory in accordance with the enemy.

Therefore,

a body of soldiers has no constant configuration; a body of water has no constant form. He who can gain victory in accordance with the transformations of the enemy is called daemonic.

Therefore,

the five phases[7] have no constant[8] victor; the four seasons have no constant status. Sunlight may be long or short; moonglow waxes and wanes.

CHAPTER 7

The Struggle of Armies

The main topics of this chapter are how to forestall the enemy by securing the conditions for victory and by setting up a superior situation from which to do battle. Essentially, it is a question of jockeying for advantage. One of the primary tenets of the Sun Zi *is enshrined here in the famous dictum that "War is premised upon deception."*

Master Sun said,

In general, the method of waging war is such that the general receives his mandate from the ruler, then assembles the masses of his army, after which he encamps, facing off against the enemy. Nothing is more difficult than the struggle of armies that ensues. The difficulty of the struggle of armies lies in taking the circuitous as straight, in taking what is troublesome to be advantageous.

Therefore,

take a circuitous route to reach the enemy, tempt him with advantages. Though I set out after him, I reach my destination before him. This is the planning of one who knows how to make the circuitous straight.[1]

Therefore,

the struggle of armies may be advantageous, but it may also be dangerous. If one commits his entire army to the struggle for advantage, he will not attain it. If one abandons all but the light components of his army in the struggle for advantage, he will forfeit his heavy equipment wagons and grain carts.

For this reason,

if he has his men roll up their armor and rush forward, not stopping day or night and doing double stages in a forced march, traveling a hundred tricents in the struggle for advantage, the generals of his three armies will be captured. Those who are vigorous will arrive first, while those who are weary will come along later, with the result that only one-tenth of the men will reach their destination. If one has his men travel fifty tricents in the contestation of advantage, the general of his upper army will fall, and the result will be that only half of his men will reach their destination. If one has his men travel thirty tricents in the struggle for advantage, two-thirds of them will reach their destination.[2]

For this reason,

if an army has no heavy equipment wagons, it will lose; if it has no grain supplies, it will lose; and if it has no provisions, it will lose.

Therefore,

he who does not know the intentions of the feudal lords should not enter into diplomatic associations with them; he who does not know the forms of the mountains and forests, the precipices and obstacles, the marshes and swamps should not march his army. He who does not employ local guides will not be able to gain the advantages of the terrain.

Therefore,

war is premised upon deception, motivated by advantage, and modified by dividing and joining.

Therefore,

his armies may be swift as the wind, calm as a forest, raging as a fire, immobile as a mountain, unfathomable as the darkness, volatile as thunder and lightning. When pillaging villages, divide the spoils among the masses; when expanding one's territory, divide the benefits. Ponder and weigh before moving.

He who is the first to know the planning of how to make the circuitous straight will be victorious.[3] This is the method of the struggle of armies.

In the *Army Administration*[4] it says, "In battle words cannot be heard, therefore gongs and drums are used; hand signals cannot be seen, therefore flags and banners are employed." Gongs, drums, flags, and banners are the means whereby the eyes and ears of men are unified. Once one's men are concentrated as one, the brave will not go forward alone, and the cowardly will not retreat alone. This is the method of using the masses.

Therefore,

in night battles fire and drums are more often used; in day battles flags and banners are often used. These are the means whereby adjustments are made for the eyes and ears of one's men.

Therefore,

the three armies can be robbed of their spirit, the general can be robbed of his resolve.[5]

For this reason,

in the morning an army's spirit is keen, by midday it begins to slacken, and by evening it is depleted.[6]

Therefore,

he who is skilled at waging war avoids the enemy army when it is in keen spirit and strikes when its spirit slackens and is depleted—this is how to control morale. Confront chaos with control; confront clamor with quietude—this is how to control the heart. Confront those who have come from a distance with one's own forces nearby;[7] confront those who have toiled with those who are rested; confront those who are hungry with those who are full—this is how to control strength. Do not challenge flags[8] that are well ordered; do not strike at formations that are well aligned—this is how to control change.

Therefore,

the method of waging war holds thus: do not face an enemy who occupies the heights; do not oppose an enemy whose back is against a hill; do not follow an enemy who feigns retreat; do not attack soldiers who are in keen spirits; do not swallow troops that the enemy offers as bait; do not intercept an army that is returning home; be sure to leave an opening for an army that is surrounded;[9] do not press a desperate foe. This is the method of waging war.

CHAPTER 8

Nine[1] Varieties[2]

This chapter addresses the question of responding deftly to contingencies and advises awareness of both the advantages and the disadvantages of any action that might be contemplated. The principle of preparedness is proposed as the surest way to avoid disaster.

Master Sun said,

The method of waging war is ordinarily that the general receives a mandate from the ruler, then assembles the army and brings together the masses. He does not encamp on unfavorable terrain; he joins with allies at terrain having a crossroads; he does not linger on forsaken terrain; he devises plans to extricate his forces from surrounded terrain; if he finds himself on desperate terrain he does battle.

There are paths that he does not take; there are armies that he does not strike; there are cities that he does not attack; there are terrains that he does not contest; there are ruler's orders that he does not accept.[3]

Therefore,

the general who is versed in the advantages[4] of the nine varieties of terrain[5] knows how to wage war; the general who is not versed in the advantages of the nine varieties, although he may know the types of terrain, cannot gain the advantages of the terrain. If one prosecutes war without knowing the techniques of the nine varieties, although one may know the five advantages,[6] one will not be able to gain the use of one's men.

For this reason,

in his considerations, he who is wise must pay attention both to advantage and to disadvantage. By paying attention to advantage, his affairs will proceed with assurance; by paying attention to disadvantage, his troubles will be resolved.

For this reason,

that which causes the feudal lords to submit is disadvantage; that which causes the feudal lords to serve is encumbrance; that which causes the feudal lords to give allegiance is advantage.

Therefore,

the method of waging war is not to rely upon the enemy's not coming, but to rely upon my waiting in readiness for him; it is not to rely upon the enemy's not attacking, but to rely upon making myself invulnerable to attack.

Therefore,

there are five fatal flaws in a general: recklessness, for he may be killed by the enemy; timidity, for he may be captured by the enemy; irascibility, for he may be provoked by the enemy; incorruptibility, for he may be insulted by the enemy; solicitousness, for he may be made anxious by the enemy. In all of these respects, if a general overdoes them, it will be disastrous for waging war. The overthrow of an enemy and the killing of a general are the inevitable consequences of these five fatal flaws. They cannot be left unexamined.[7]

CHAPTER 9

Marching the Army

The present chapter deals with the orders of march for an army but also touches on methods for observing enemy forces and determining the significance of the circumstances of the opposing army. A key issue considered here is how to effectively combine the civil (wen) and the martial (wu).

Master Sun said,

In the placement of one's army and in the scrutiny[1] of the enemy, the following ordinarily apply: in cutting through mountains stick to the valleys; place the army on a height looking toward the sun;[2] when battling at an elevation do not advance upwards toward the enemy—these are rules for the placement of an army in the mountains. Before crossing a river, the army must be placed at a distance from the water;[3] when the enemy is crossing a river toward you, do not meet him in the water; let half the enemy forces get across and then strike, for this will be to your advantage; if you wish to do battle with the enemy, do not meet him close to the water; place the army on a height looking toward the sun, and do not advance upstream toward the enemy—these are rules for the placement of an army near the water. When cutting across marshes and swamps, it is essential to get out of them quickly and not to linger; if you want to join battle with the enemy army in swamps and marshes, you must stick to the grasses and keep your back to the woods—these are rules for the placement of an army in swamps and marshes. In the plains, place the army on level ground but with its rear against the higher ground above[4] it, the lowlands in front and the uplands behind[5]—these are rules for the placement of an army in the plains. The advantages of these four types of placement of an army are such that the Yellow Emperor[6] used them to vanquish the Four Emperors.[7]

An army ordinarily likes heights and dislikes depths, values brightness and disparages darkness, nourishes itself on vitality and places itself on solidity. Thus it will not fall prey to a host of ailments and may be declared "invincible." When setting up defensive earthworks on hills and ridges, the general must place his army on the sunny side with its rear against the higher ground above it. These military advantages are support that is derived from the terrain.

When there is rain upstream and frothy waters reach you, if you wish to have your army ford the river, you should wait until the flood has abated.

Wherever the terrain takes the following forms, you must leave as quickly as possible and not get near them: Cleft Ravine, Sky Wall, Sky Corral, Sky Net, Sky Sink, Sky Crevice.[8] I distance myself from these forms and let the enemy get near them; I face these forms and let my enemy have his back next to them.

When marching one's army, where there are precipices and obstacles, reed-filled depressions, and mountain forests with dense foliage, you must thread your way through them with utmost caution, for these are places where ambushes and snipers are found.

When the enemy is nearby but remains still, it is because he is relying on his strategic location; when he is far off but tries to incite me into battle, it is because he wants me to advance. If he chooses to occupy a place that is easily accessible, it must be because he finds some advantage there.

When the multitude of trees begin to move,[9] the enemy is coming; when there are many screens among the multitude of grasses, the enemy is trying to sow doubt; when birds fly up, there is an ambush. When animals run away frightened, the enemy intends to overwhelm me.[10]

When dust rises sharply upward, chariots are coming; when it hangs low and spreads out broadly, foot soldiers are coming; when it is long and wispy, the enemy is gathering firewood; when it is small and sporadic, the enemy is searching for a place to set up camp. When the enemy's envoys employ obsequious language, his preparations are intensifying, and he is getting ready to advance; when the enemy's language is aggressive and he makes a show of rushing forward, he is getting ready to retreat; when the enemy's light chariots appear first and occupy the sides, he will have his troops go into formation; when he sues for peace without any prior agreement, he is scheming; when he races forward with his soldiers and chariots fully deployed, he seeks to engage in battle with me; when he partially advances and partially retreats, he is trying to tempt me. If the enemy's soldiers lean on their weapons while standing, they are hungry; if they drink first when filling vessels with water, they are thirsty; if they see advantage but do not advance toward it, they are weary. If birds flock to the enemy camp, that means it is empty; if the enemy soldiers call out in the night, it means they are terrified; if there is turmoil in the enemy camp, the commander is insufficiently stern; if their flags and banners are moving, there is chaos; if the officers are irritable, they are tired; if they feed their horses grain and eat the flesh of their animals, the army has taken down the cooking pots from their hooks and will not return to their camp—they are in desperate straits. If the enemy soldiers cluster together and talk to each other slowly and earnestly in low voices, it means that the general has lost their trust; if the enemy is profligate in handing out rewards, it means that he is in extremity; if he is overly harsh with his punishments, it means that he is in straightened circumstances; if their general first treats his men cruelly and then later fears them, he is utterly lacking in perspicacity; if enemy envoys come under a pretext to seek terms, it means they want to cease hostilities. If the enemy forces angrily advance and confront us but wait long without engaging in battle, I must cautiously examine their aims.

War is not a matter of the more troops the better. So long as one does not advance rashly, concentrates his strength, and understands[11] his enemy, that will suffice to take the foe. But if one is not circumspect and treats the enemy lightly, he will surely be captured by his foe.

If one punishes his troops before he has gained their fealty, they will not submit to him, and if they do not submit it will be difficult to use them in battle; if one has already gained the fealty of troops but does not carry out appropriate punishments, he cannot use them in battle either.

Therefore,

I cultivate my soldiers with civility[12] and treat them even-handedly according to military regulations. Hence I will be sure to achieve my goal. If all along I can ensure that my orders are carried out so that my men are properly instructed, then my men will submit; if all along I cannot ensure that my orders are carried out so that my men are properly instructed, then my men will not submit. The reason I can ensure that my orders are carried out all along is that there is mutual trust between me and my multitudes.

CHAPTER 10

Terrain Types[1]

In this chapter, the principles for moving an army across different types of terrain are discussed. Emphasis is placed on the study of topography and on utilizing it to one's advantage. Also stressed extremely heavily is the sheer value of awareness of the real situation, with the verb zhi *("know") occurring thirteen times.[2]*

Master Sun said,

There are the following types of terrain: accessible, hanging, branching, narrow, precarious, distant. The type through which I can go and my opponent can come is called "accessible." On the accessible type of terrain, if I am the first to occupy the sunny heights and facilitate the routes for grain supply, this will be advantageous in battle. The type through which I can go but from which it is difficult to return is called "hanging." On the hanging type of terrain, if the enemy is not prepared, I may go forth and conquer him; but if the enemy is prepared and I go forth, I will not conquer him; it is not advantageous for me. The type through which it is neither advantageous for me nor for the enemy to go forth is called "branching." On the branching type of terrain, although the enemy may tempt me with advantage, I should not go forth; rather, I should lead my troops in a feigned withdrawal, inducing the enemy to come forth partially, upon which I should strike him. On the narrow type of terrain, if I occupy it first, I should fill it and await the enemy; if the enemy occupies it first and fills it, I should not enter it, but if he has not filled it, I should enter it. On the precarious type of terrain, if I occupy it first, I should occupy the sunny heights and await the enemy; if the enemy occupies it first, I should lead my troops in withdrawal and not enter it. On the distant type of terrain, if our configurations are comparable, it is difficult for either side to provoke the other to battle; if I do battle, it will not be advantageous for me. These six cases are all illustrations of the way of utilizing the terrain; comprehending them is an important responsibility of the general—they cannot be left unexamined.

Therefore,

there are the following different types of forces: put to flight, lax, depressed, collapsed, chaotic, routed. In all of these six cases, it is not a matter of a natural disaster, but the fault of the general. If the configurations of the two opponents are comparable, but if one opponent only uses one-tenth of his forces, they will be put to flight. If one's troops are strong but his officers are weak, his army will be lax. If one's officers are strong but his troops are weak, his army will be depressed. If one's high officers are full of fury and their general does not rein them in, when they encounter the enemy they will seethe with resentment and do battle on their own initiative; the general not knowing his own ability to stop them, the army will collapse. If a general is weak and lacks sternness, if his precepts are not clear, and if the officers and troops have no constant regulations, their formations will be disordered, and the army will be chaotic. If a general, not understanding the enemy, joins in battle against a multitude with a small number of troops, striking the strong with the weak, and his forces lack a select vanguard, they will be routed. These six cases are all illustrations of the way of defeat; comprehending them is an important responsibility of the general—they cannot be left unexamined.

The types of terrain are a potential source of support in warfare. Understanding the enemy and creating the conditions for victory, calculating danger and distance—this is the way of the top general. He who engages in battle knowing these things will surely be victorious; he who engages in battle not knowing these things will surely be defeated.

Therefore,

if a battle is materializing in such a way that one will surely be victorious, yet one's sovereign tells one not to do battle, one can persist with the battle; if a battle is materializing in such a way that one will not be victorious, yet one's sovereign says that one must do battle, one can desist from the battle.

Therefore,

when advancing do not seek fame; when retreating do not shun culpability. Strive to protect the people and to do what is compatible with the best interests of one's sovereign. A general like this is a state treasure.

Look upon the troops as infants.
Therefore,
you will be able to lead them through deep ravines.

Look upon the troops as beloved sons.
Therefore,
you will be able to have them follow you to the death.[3]

But if you are overly generous to the troops, you will not be able to depute them; if you dote upon the troops, you will not be able to order them; if you let them behave without discipline, you will not be able to control them. Like spoiled children, such troops cannot be used.

If I only know that my troops can strike but do not know that the enemy cannot be struck, I have only fulfilled half of the conditions for victory. If I know that the enemy can be struck but do not know that my troops cannot strike, I have only fulfilled half of the conditions for victory. If I know that the enemy can be struck and know that my troops can strike, but do not know that the type of terrain is such that I cannot do battle on it, I have only fulfilled half of the conditions for battle.

Therefore,
he who knows warfare moves without confusion, acts without constraint.

Therefore,
it is said, "If you know your opponent and you know yourself,[4] victory will not be at risk; if you know heaven and you know earth,[5] your victories will be unlimited."

CHAPTER 11

Nine Types of Terrain

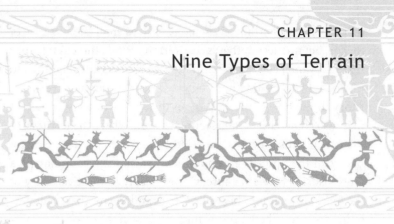

By far the longest in the Sun Zi, this chapter takes up yet again the question of different types of terrain. Here, however, the emphasis is more upon how to use one's forces on different kinds of land than upon the different landforms themselves. Nonetheless, the tremendous amount of attention paid to topography in the Sun Zi certifies that this was a central concern of those who were responsible for the compilation. Aside from landforms, this chapter also notes the paramount importance of speed in military operations and the need for directing one's forces toward a particular point in the enemy's defenses, rather than indiscriminately spreading them across a broad front.

Master Sun said,

According to the method of waging war, there are the following types of terrain:[1] dispersed, easy, contested, intersecting, having a crossroads, encumbered, unfavorable, surrounded, desperate. When the feudal lords battle the enemy on their own territory, that is dispersed terrain.[2] When one's forces enter the territory of the foe, but not deeply, that is easy terrain. When there is territory that is advantageous to me if I take it but is also advantageous to my foe if he takes it, that is contested terrain. When there is territory through which I may go but through which my opponent may also come, that is intersecting terrain. Where the territory of the feudal lords is triply connected,[3] and where the first to arrive may gain the hosts of all under heaven, that is terrain having a crossroads. Where one's forces enter deeply into the territory of the foe and are next to his walled cities and towns, that is encumbered terrain. Where one's armies must march[4] through mountains and forests, precipices and obstacles, marshes and swamps, wherever the way makes for a difficult march, that is unfavorable terrain. Where the entrance is narrow and exit is circuitous, and where the foe can strike my hosts with a small number of troops, that is surrounded terrain. Where my army will survive if we quickly do battle but will perish if we hesitate, that is desperate terrain.

For this reason,

I do not do battle on dispersed terrain;[5] I do not linger on easy terrain; I do not attack on contested terrain; I do not break off communications on intersecting terrain; I maintain diplomatic linkages on terrain having a crossroads; I pillage on encumbered terrain; I march swiftly through unfavorable terrain; I formulate plans on surrounded terrain; I do battle on desperate terrain.[6]

The so-called[7] ancients who were skilled at waging war could cause the men of the enemy to be unable to link up front and rear, the hosts and the smaller units to be unable to rely on each other, the nobles and the commoners to be unable to aid each other, the superiors and inferiors to be unable to cohere, the troops to separate and be unable to regroup, the soldiers who come together to do so unevenly.[8]

When an action is advantageous, take it; when an action is disadvantageous, refrain from it.

I make bold to ask, "If the enemy hosts are well ordered and about to come toward us, how should we await them?" Answer: "First snatch away that which they are most fond of,[9] then they will be more tractable."[10]

The circumstances of warfare put a premium on speed, so that one may take his opponent unawares by a route he is not expecting, attacking him when he is ill-prepared.

The way of a "guest"[11] army is to enter deeply into the territory of the enemy and to concentrate one's forces so that the "host"[12] may not "conquer the guest." Pillage in the rich countryside, so that the three armies will have enough to eat. Carefully nourish your soldiers and do not make them weary, so that they may conserve their energy and build up their strength. When you put your forces in motion, do so with calculated planning, so that the enemy will not be able to discern your aims.

Throw your forces into positions from which there is no outlet; there they may die, but they will not be put to rout. Since they are ready for death, the officers and men will exert themselves to the utmost. The soldiers and their officers will fear no pitfall whatever, so no matter where they go they will hold firm. Though they may enter deep into enemy territory, they will maintain their resolve and fight to the end if there is no other alternative.

For this reason,

such forces will be vigilant even without drilling; will fulfill their duties without being importuned; will assist each other without being compelled; will be trustworthy without being ordered. If you prohibit talk of omens and banish doubts, the troops will go anywhere, even unto death.

My officers getting rid of their extra belongings is not because they detest material goods; their willingness to give up the remainder of their allotted life span is not because they detest longevity. On the day when the order to set forth to war is issued, one's officers and troops may sit weeping till their lapels are soaked with tears, and they may lie on their backs with tears streaming down their cheeks. But when you throw them into positions from which there is no outlet, they will be as brave as Zhuan Zhu and Cao Gui.[13]

Therefore,

he who is skilled at waging war may be compared to Shuairan. Shuairan is the name of a snake that lives on Mt. Heng.[14] If you strike its head, the tail will come at you; if you strike its tail, the head will come at you; if you strike it in the middle, both the head and the tail will come at you.[15]

I make bold to ask, "Can armed forces be made to behave like Shuairan?" Answer: "Yes. The people of Wu and the people of Yue dislike each other, but if they encounter a storm when crossing a river in the same boat, they will help each other like someone's left and right hand."[16]

For this reason,

if you tether your horses in lines and bury the wheels of your chariots in the soil, this is not a reliable method for keeping them in formation. If you want your brave warriors to act in concert as one, it is a matter of exercising leadership; to make the most of both the hard and the soft, it is a question of utilizing the different types of terrain.

Therefore,

he who is skilled at waging war leads his army by the hand as easily as if he were dispatching a single person. It is because he places them in a situation where they have no alternative but to act in unison.[17]

Generalship requires calmness and reserve, correctness and control. The general should stupefy[18] the eyes and ears of his officers and troops, so that they will have no knowledge.[19] Change your affairs, alter your plans, so that the people will have no recognition.[20] Change your dwelling, make your path circuitous, so that the people will not be concerned about them.

If the commander has an agreement with his army, it is as though they climbed high up and he pulled the ladder out from under them.[21] When he leads his army deep into the territory of the feudal lords, he releases his men as though he were pulling the trigger[22] of a crossbow. He burns his army's boats and destroys their cauldrons.[23] He drives them as if they were a herd of goats; he drives them this way and that, but they know not where they are going. He assembles the hosts of his three armies and throws them into precarious places; this is the business of a general.

The nine types of terrain, the advantages of expanding and contracting, the principles of human emotions—these cannot be left unexamined.

The way of being a "guest" is to concentrate one's forces when one has deeply entered another's territory, to disperse when one has entered shallowly.

When one leads his army out of his own kingdom and crosses over the border, he is said to have entered inaccessible terrain. Where there are thoroughfares leading in all four directions, that is terrain having a crossroads. Where one enters deeply, that is encumbered terrain. Where one enters shallowly, that is easy terrain. Where one has his back to solid landforms and it is narrow in front, that is surrounded terrain. Where there is no outlet, that is desperate terrain.

For this reason,
    on dispersed terrain I shall unify their will; on easy terrain I shall cause my troops to maintain a command structure; on contested terrain I shall rush to the rear; on intersecting terrain I shall guard it carefully; on terrain with crossroads I shall solidify my ties with the feudal lords; on encumbered terrain I shall ensure a strong supply of grain; on unfavorable terrain I shall pass along the path quickly; on surrounded terrain I shall seal up the openings; on desperate terrain I shall reveal the spirit of being ready to give up one's life.[24]

Therefore,

the emotions of one's soldiers are such that, when surrounded, they will resist the enemy; when they have no alternative, they will fight to the death; when they have crossed over into perilous territory, they will follow my commands.

For this reason,

he who does not know the plans of the feudal lords should not forge diplomatic ties with them.[25] He who does not know the forms of mountains and forests, precipices and obstacles, and marshes and swamps should not march an army. He who does not use lo cal guides cannot obtain the advantages of the different types of terrain. If one does not know the advantages and disadvantages of even a single one of the four plus five,[26] he cannot be the leader of the forces of a hegemon king. The forces of a hegemon king can chastise the great states, so that they will not be able to assemble their hosts; they can intimidate the enemy so that he will not be able to forge ties with other states.

For this reason,

do not compete in forging alliances with all under heaven, do not expand your authority throughout all under heaven. Trust in your own power and use it to intimidate the enemy.

Therefore,

you will be able to uproot his cities and destroy his state. Offer rewards that exceed the legal limits; deliver orders that go beyond administrative norms—you will be able to drive the hosts of the three armies as though you were directing a single man. Drive them to carry out tasks, but don't tell them the reasons why; drive them with advantages, but don't tell them the disadvantages—if you throw them upon forsaken terrain, they will still survive; if you sink them in desperate terrain,[27] they will still live. Even if one's hosts sink in disadvantage, they can still overcome defeat.

Therefore,
the matter of war lies in pretending to go along with the enemy's intention while directing your forces at a single spot in his perimeter. Thus you will be able to kill one of his generals, even at a distance of a thousand tricents. This is called "using cleverness to achieve great things."

For this reason,
on the day when war is declared, seal the passes and abrogate contracts. Cut off communications with the enemy's emissaries. Hone your calculations in the temple[28] in order to assess the matter at hand. If there are any gaps in the enemy's defenses, you must exploit them immediately. First occupy that which the enemy favors most; do not enter into any agreements with him. Before laying down any guidelines, adjust to the circumstances of the enemy to determine the affairs of battle.[29]

For this reason,
at the beginning be as still as a virgin, but when the enemy relaxes his guard, spring forth like a rabbit that has escaped from its cage. The enemy will not be able to put up any resistance.

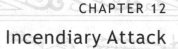

CHAPTER 12

Incendiary Attack

This chapter introduces the different types of attack by fire, the conditions necessary for using them, and the methods for carrying them out. It is of a manifestly different character from all the others in the Sun Zi, *since it is the only one that deals with actual technical aspects of a specific act of war, rather than tactics and strategy. As pointed out in the introduction, this chapter shares striking parallels with Greek writings on incendiary warfare.*

Master Sun said,

In all there are five different kinds of incendiary attack. They are to use fire against: 1. men,[1] 2. grain, 3. carts,[2] 4. storehouses, 5. supply lines. If one wishes to carry out an incendiary attack, all of the conditions must be right, and one must always keep a supply of incendiary materials on hand. There are suitable times and suitable days for launching incendiary attacks. The suitable times are when it is dry, and the suitable days are "Winnowing Basket,"

"Wall," "Wing," and "Carriage Crossboard." The times when the moon is in one of these four lunar lodges[3] are the days when the wind blows strongly.

In making an incendiary attack, one must ordinarily complement it with military force. When the fire is burning inside the enemy camp, one should complement it with military force from outside as soon as possible. If the fire has already broken out but the enemy soldiers remain quiet, one should wait before attacking. When the fire has reached a peak, one may follow up with an assault if that is suitable, but if it is not suitable, refrain from an assault.

If a fire can be set from outside, you need not wait until it can be set from inside, but simply set it in a timely fashion. If the fire has been set upwind, do not attack from downwind. If a wind blows for a long time during the day, it will stop at night. An army must in all cases understand the five different varieties of incendiary attacks and stay on guard until the criteria for setting them obtain.

Therefore,
   Supporting one's attack with fire yields obvious results; supporting one's attack with water[4] yields impressive results. Water can break up enemy forces, but, unlike fire, it cannot deprive the enemy of his matériel.

To be victorious in battle and to take the enemy's holdings through attack, but to refrain from building on your accomplishments is baleful: this may be termed a wasted opportunity.[5]

Therefore,

it is said, the perspicacious ruler is concerned about what to do with the spoils of war; the excellent general takes steps to build on them.

If there is no advantage, do not mobilize; if you cannot achieve your aims, do not go to war; if you are not endangered, do not engage in battle. The ruler should not, in a moment of anger, raise his armies; the general should not, in a burst of ire, embark upon battle. If it is compatible with the interests of the state, then mobilize; if it is not compatible with the interests of the state, then halt. If you are angry, you can be happy again; if you are full of ire, you can be joyful again. But if your state perishes, you cannot restore it; if your men die, you cannot bring them back to life.[6]

Therefore,

the perspicacious ruler is cautious; the excellent general is vigilant. This is the way of making the state secure and preserving the army intact.

CHAPTER 13

Using Spies

The last chapter stresses the importance of spies and methods for their employment. On the one hand, it offers a sensible, pragmatic view of the need for intelligence. On the other hand, the scorn it displays for superstitious and mystical methods of prediction (as opposed to the acquisition of realistic, hard data) is remarkable for its time. Judging from the style and contents, this chapter appears to have been composed much later than all of the other chapters in the Sun Zi. The extraordinary emphasis it places on espionage, particularly the employment of double agents, plus its placement as the concluding chapter, highlights the value of human intelligence for military operations.

Master Sun said,

Whenever a hundred thousand troops are raised and sent on an expedition a thousand tricents away, the expenditures of the common people and the contributions from public funds amount to a thousand pieces of gold per day. Inside and outside there is much turmoil; people exhaust themselves on the roads; and 700,000 households cannot attend to their agricultural and other daily chores.[1] The warring parties may face off for several years to contest for the victory of a single day. And yet there are those who, out of niggardliness for their rank and salary, are unwilling to spend a hundred pieces of gold on spies: this is the height of inhumanity![2] A general like this is not a general of the people, nor is he of assistance to his lord, and a lord like this is not destined for victory.

Therefore,

the reason the perspicacious lord and the wise general are victorious over others when they mobilize and the reason their meritorious accomplishments exceed those of the masses is their foreknowledge.[3] Foreknowledge is something that cannot be gotten from ghosts and spirits, nor can it be obtained from interpreting the symbols of things,[4] nor can it be acquired through astrological verification. Foreknowledge must be gained through people, specifically those who know the circumstances of the enemy.

Therefore,

there are five different types of spies that may be put to use: those who have an excuse, inside agents, double agents, those who risk death, and those who escape with their lives. If these five types are employed simultaneously, the enemy will not be able to keep himself informed of their hidden ways. This is the so-called "miraculous conduct" of spies, the treasure of the ruler of men.

Spies who have an excuse are drawn from the local people among the enemy. Inside agents are drawn from the officials of the enemy. Double agents are drawn from the agents of the enemy. Spies who risk death do so because we disseminate false information, letting it be known to our agents who spread it to the enemy agents.[5] Spies who escape with their lives are those who return to make a report.

Therefore,

among the affairs of the three armies, there is no one more intimate than the spy, no one who receives heavier rewards than the spy, and no one who is more secretive than the spy. Only the sage and wise know how to make use of spies; only the humane and just know how to employ spies; only the subtle and sensitive know how to extract genuine intelligence from spies. Subtle indeed! There is nowhere that one may not use spies, but if the plans based upon information provided by spies are divulged before they have been launched, then both the spy and those to whom he has told it will be killed.[6]

If there is any army I wish to strike, any city I wish to attack, any person I wish to kill, I must first know the names and surnames of the defending general, his trusted associates, the appointment secretary, the gatekeepers, his retainers, then order my spies to find out as much as they can about them. I must further seek out the enemy agents who come to spy on us, ply them with benefits, induce them to come over to our side, and then release them back to the enemy.

Therefore,

I will have gained double agents who are at my disposal. Consequently, I will know more about the enemy and will therefore be able to acquire spies who have an excuse and inside agents whom I will be able to employ. Consequently, I will know still more about the enemy and will therefore be able to send spies who risk death to disseminate false information among the enemy. Consequently, I will know yet more about the enemy and will therefore be able to have my spies who escape with their lives return at the appointed time.

The lord must be well informed about the affairs of the five different kinds of agents, and his ability to be kept well informed necessarily depends upon double agents.

Therefore,
he cannot but give his double agents the heaviest rewards.

Of old, when the Yin Dynasty[7] arose, it made use of Yi Zhi, who had formerly served the Xia; when the Zhou Dynasty arose, it made use of Lü Ya, who had formerly served the Yin.[8]

Therefore,
the perspicacious ruler and the wise general who can make those of high intelligence be their spies will certainly have great accomplishments. This is the essence of warfare, and it is that which the three armies depend upon in order to take action.

The Pseudo-Biography of Sun Wu

Below is a complete translation of the "biography" of Sun Zi from the Shi ji
(The Grand Scribe's Records), *s. 65. Written by Sima Qian (145–ca. 86 B.C.)
around the year 97 B.C., it is an essentially fictional account of a figure for
whom there is no other more secure information.*

Master Sun, whose courtesy name was Wu ("Martial"), was
a man of Qi.[1] Because of his *bingfa,*[2] he gained audience with
Helu,[3] the king of Wu.[4] Helu said to him, "I have read the whole
of your thirteen chapters.[5] Can you give me a small demonstration of how you train soldiers?" Master Sun replied, "Yes, I can."
Helu asked, "Can you do the demonstration with women?"
Master Sun replied, "Yes, I can."

Thereupon it was permitted for one hundred and eighty
beauties to be brought out of the palace. Master Sun divided
the women into two companies, with two of the king's favored
concubines as company commanders, and he ordered all of
them to carry halberds.

Master Sun gave them orders, "Do you know where your
heart and back, your left hand and right hand are?" The women

replied, "We know." Master Sun said, "If I want you to go forward, face in the direction of your heart. If I want you to go to the left, face in the direction of your left hand. If I want you to go to the right, face in the direction of your right hand. If I want you to go to the rear, face in the direction of your back." "Yes, sir!" replied the women.

The marching commands having been proclaimed, Master Sun had a large battle-ax brought out, then he repeated the orders over and over.[6]

Thereupon Master Sun drummed[7] them to the right, and the women broke out in laughter. Master Sun said, "If the marching commands are not clear, and if the orders have not been repeated enough to make them familiar, that is the fault of the general."

Again, Master Sun repeated the orders over and over, then he drummed them to the left, and again the women broke out in laughter. Master Sun said, "If the marching commands are not clear, and if the orders have not been repeated enough to make them familiar, that is the fault of the general. Since the commands have already been made clear, yet you do not execute them according to the regulations, that is the fault of your officers."

Whereupon, he wished to execute the left and right company commanders. When the king of Wu, who was observing the proceedings from a terrace, saw that his concubines were about to be executed, he was greatly terrified. Hastily, he sent a messenger to deliver the following order: "We already realize that you know how to conduct military operations, general. If we, however, are bereft of these two concubines, our food will be tasteless. We hope that you will not execute them."

Master Sun said, "Since your servant has already received your command to be the general of your army, and I am now with the army, 'there are ruler's orders that he does not accept.'"[8]

Whereupon he had the two company commanders executed[9] as a warning to the others.

After he appointed the next two in line to be the company commanders, he again drummed the soldiers. The women turned to the left and right, went forward and backward, knelt and rose as precisely as if their movements had been measured with a compass and L-square. None of them dared make a sound. Thereupon, Master Sun sent a messenger to report to the king: "The soldiers are now in perfect order. Your Honor may come down and observe them. They will do whatever Your Honor wishes, even if you want them to go through fire and water." The king of Wu said, "Enough, general! You may return to your quarters. I do not wish to come down and observe."

Master Sun said, "Your Honor only cherishes the words of the *bingfa,* but cannot apply their reality."

Thereupon, Helu came to realize that Master Sun was capable of conducting military operations, and eventually made him a general.[10] Subsequently, the kingdom of Wu destroyed the powerful state of Chu[11] to the west, entering its capital at Ying,[12] awed the states of Qi and Jin[13] to the north, and achieved illustrious fame among the feudal lords. Master Sun played an important role in all of these developments.[14]

On the whole, this is not a very helpful introduction to the putative author of the *Sun Zi* and his career. Indeed, the only useful information in it appears in the first and last paragraphs, both of which are short. From these two paragraphs, we learn that Master Sun was supposedly a native of Qi, which was in the northeast of what is now China (the modern province of Shandong), that he was granted an audience with the king of Wu (a coastal state that lay to the south of the Yangtze), and that he later served as a commander in the Wu army. The rest of the quasi biography, more than four-fifths of the whole, is taken up with a highly improbable, blood-curdling account of Master Sun drilling 180 palace beauties and ruthlessly beheading the king's two most favored ladies. Sima Qian, though, certainly did not fabricate this story, since it is told at still greater length in one of the Yinque Shan bamboo strip manuscripts that was found with the *Sun Zi,* namely, the fragmentary text that has been given the provisional title of "Jian Wu wang" (An audience with the king of Wu) (Yinque Shan 1976:106–8). In this earlier rendition of the tale, it is Master Sun who offers to use "noble persons . . . , ignoble persons . . . , [or] women" to demonstrate his rigorous military discipline.

From the more expansive but less polished manner of the story as it is related in the archeologically recovered manuscript version, it would appear that Sima Qian, author of the *Shi ji,* has abbreviated a preexisting legend. Inasmuch as the Yinque Shan manuscripts date to between 134 and 118 B.C., this means that the story of Master Sun's interview with King Helu was probably already in circulation by at least the first half of the second c. B.C. It also pushes back the antecedents of the thirteen-chapter edition of the *Sun Zi* to a similar time, since the extended version of the story in the bamboo strip manuscripts twice mentions that number of chapters.

For an English translation of the Yinque Shan manuscript version of this fanciful tale, see Ames (1993:191–96). The Chinese text is available in Yinque Shan Hanmu Zhujian Zhengli Xiaozu (1976:106–8, nn. 109–11).

Although Sun Wu's "biography" in *Shi ji* 65 is sorely disappointing, there is more that can be said about the scroll as a whole, for he shares it with Sun Bin (and thereby hangs a tale), not to mention Wu Qi (and thereby hangs another tale). See the introduction for a complete translation of the biography of Sun Bin and for additional information concerning Wu Qi, with whom Sun Zi is often paired.

1. (Initial) Assessments

The first character of this title was added by later editors. Originally, the title of this chapter consisted of only a single character. The same is true of the titles of chapters four and five, whereas all the other chapters of the Sun Zi consist of two characters.

1. The word rendered here as "assessments" (*ji*) also includes the notion of "calculations, schemes, stratagems, plans," and so forth. The overall gist implied by its use in *Sun Zi* is that successful designs for war can only be achieved when the actual situation is accurately evaluated. Indeed, so vital is precise accounting of the circumstances one faces that it is tantamount to victory. Conversely, inexact stocktaking inevitably leads to defeat. Hence, realistic appraisal and strategic planning go hand in hand, with the latter premised upon the former.

2. As in the *Mo Zi* and other Warring States texts, the obligatory opening formula, "Master X said," is a fair indication that the *Sun Zi* was not written by the putative Master Sun himself.

3. This is the highly multivalent term *bing*, for which see the section "Key Terms."

4. *Zuo zhuan*, Duke Cheng 13: "The great affairs of the state are sacrifice and war." Although this is how the *Zuo zhuan* statement is almost universally understood, the context indicates more precisely that it should be interpreted as, "The great affairs of state reside in the temple sacrifice and in the war sacrifice." (Shaughnessy 1996:159)

5. Li Quan: "War is an instrument of evil omen. Life and death, preservation and destruction are tied to it. That is why it is considered a weighty matter—out of fear that men will engage in it lightly." *Tao te ching/Dao de jing* 31: "Weapons are instruments of evil omen; Creation abhors them."

6. This clause in the original text lacks the number seven, but since there are seven assessments mentioned in the succession of sentences below that begin with the interrogative "Which," and since the parallel clause above has a numeral in the corresponding position, it is fitting to add it here.

7. This is not the metaphysical entity of early Taoist discourse nor the ethical and cosmological construct of Confucian thought. Rather, in the *Sun Zi*, it is a more practical, methodological notion.

8. Coming as it does immediately after Tao (*dao*, the Way), it is easy for *tian* to be interpreted as "Heaven," but we shall see that later in the *Sun Zi* it often means "Nature."

9. Because it comes immediately after *tian* ("Heaven"), it is easy to render *di* as "Earth," but elsewhere in the *Sun Zi* it usually refers to the physical ground upon which war is fought, hence "terrain" or "topography."

10. Specifically the ruler. Cf. *Xun Zi*, "A Discussion of War": "Therefore, the essential thing about war lies in being good at gaining the support of the people." This also reminds us of the three chapters (11–13) in the *Mo Zi* that are entitled "Identifying with One's Superior" (A, B, C). There is, however, a dissenting view that the expression *shang tong* in the title of these chapters means "Valuing Unity."

11. For this last clause, the Yinque Shan manuscript has *min fu gui ye* ("the people will not go against him").

12. But here generally understood as signifying night and day, clear or overcast, and so forth.

13. Or winter and summer.

14. The passage of the seasons.

15. The Yinque Shan manuscript adds *gao xia* ("high or deep") before "broad or narrow" at the beginning of this rearranged series of topographical qualities, and the other three pairs follow in succession.

16. That is, positions conducive to survival or death. In later chapters dealing with the terrain, "death" signifies the placement of troops in desperate topographical circumstances and "life" its opposite.

17. The ruler.

18. Because the first character (*jiang*) of this sentence can mean either "general" or "(if) . . . will," and because the subjects of most (possibly all) of the verbs are unspecified, there are several radically different interpretations possible. One alternative is, "If you (i.e., the ruler) will employ the general who listens to my assessments, you will certainly be victorious, so you should retain him; if you (i.e., the ruler) will employ the general who doesn't listen to my assessments, you will certainly be defeated, so you should send him away." There are still other possible interpretations, but none make quite as much sense as the one adopted here, despite the fact that (like the others) it presents a few grammatical challenges.

    Zhang Yu lamely closes his commentary on this difficult sentence by stating that, "with these words, Master Sun is [trying] to stimulate the king of Wu and thereby seek employment."

19. One of the most important concepts in the *Sun Zi, shi* is also an extremely elusive idea. Master Sun himself must have been aware of this, since in the next sentence he attempts (not very successfully) to define it. See the notes on "Key Terms" and chap. 5 for further discussion.

    Cao Cao: "Outside the regular methods." Mei Yaochen: "Settle [your] assessments within and create a favorable configuration without, in order to achieve victory."

20. Another slippery, yet essential, concept in the *Sun Zi* is *quan*, which conveys an array of meanings that range from "power" to "authority," "right," "flexibility," "initiative," "expediency," "adaptability," "estimation,"

"opportune moment," "tactical balance of power," and "advantageous position" (in the last sense showing its close kinship to *shi*).

21. The form of the statement is such that the following translation would also be warranted: "Warfare may be defined as a way of deception."

22. This is one of the most frequently quoted maxims of the *Sun Zi*, but it is by no means a unique view, since Kauṭilya, Machiavelli, and many others subscribe to a similar outlook. Furthermore, not everyone would agree with the viewpoint advocated here. For example, the *bingfa* in the *Guan Zi* (ca. 250 B.C.) asserts:

> To destroy the large and vanquish the strong is [the way] to achieve having only one [battle]. / To throw them into disorder without resorting to opportunism, to gain ascendancy over them without resorting to deception, and to vanquish them without resorting to treachery is [the way] to realize having only one [battle].   (Rickett 1985:277)

Instead of "deception" and "treachery," the *bingfa* in the *Guan Zi* advocates overwhelming strength through mastery of tactics, training of forces, and refinement of weapons.

23. Giving or presenting an appearance that is at odds with the reality that pertains to oneself is, in essence, to pretend. This is a central tenet in the type of psychological warfare advocated by the *Sun Zi*.

24. These two identical clauses are to be found in *Sun Bin* (chap. 3, "The Questions of King Wei"), though in an entirely different context. This is good evidence that there was a body of military lore that circulated widely during the Warring States period and that could be drawn upon freely by diverse strategists and thinkers.

25. This temple is not a religious institution, but the inner sanctum within the palace precincts where the ruler made the most important decisions of state in consultation with his most trusted advisers. Cf. *Huainan Zi*, "A Discussion on Military Strategy": "Therefore, by manipulating counting rods in the temple hall, one can determine victory a thousand tricents away." "Temple computations" refers to taking stock before engaging in battle, the temple being comparable

to what today might be called a war room. What the *Sun Zi* is advocating in this passage is the careful evaluation of one's matériel and overall preparedness ahead of embarking upon a campaign. The "counting rods" to which the *Sun Zi* refers constitute criteria for success. The same usage occurs in *Sun Bin* (see the next note).

26. *Sun Bin* 20, "The Statuses of Guest (Invader) and Host (Defender)": "Will the one with the larger number [of troops necessarily] win? If so, [we can determine the outcome of] battle by laying out our counting rods." Coupled with the emphasis on assessment and calculation that began this chapter, the stress on computation with which it ends makes one feel that, for the authors of the *Sun Bin*, war—at least in its preliminary stages—was a matter that very much concerned people with the minds and abilities of accountants and actuaries. This type of calculation and assessment before battle is quite different from the divination and prognostication that were prevalent during the Spring and Autumn period and before.

2. Doing Battle

1. Used for making and maintaining bows, arrows, and other apparatus, but here standing for a broad range of military supplies in general.
2. "*Quickly*" being understood.
3. Du Mu: "The *Guan Zi* (ca. 250 B.C.) says, 'Transporting grain 300 tricents results in the loss of one year's stock; transporting grain 400 tricents results in the loss of two years' stock; transporting grain 500 tricents results in the masses having a hungry look.'"
4. This term usually designates the region of the middle course of the Yellow River, but here it means merely "in the country back home."
5. A measure of weight equal to roughly sixty-six pounds at the time the *Sun Zi* was compiled.
6. This is in sharp contrast to a modern professional approach to soldiery whereby the fighting men are aware of the strategic purpose for which they engage in combat, and are forbidden to loot.

7. Changing colors is a common theme in accounts of warfare of the Warring States period. During earlier periods, one more often hears of the mass slaughter of the captured foe, particularly those who were border peoples. The amount of the slain enemy was counted by slicing off the ears of the corpses and presenting them to one's superiors, since bringing back the severed heads of thousands of the annihilated foe would have been too heavy.

8. Meng: "Value a swift victory and a speedy return." Mei Yaochen: "Swiftness saves expenses and materials, and spares the people's labor."

3. Planning for the Attack

1. Lau (1965:333–34) proposes the alternative rendering of "preserve" or "preserving" for "take" or "taking" throughout this passage.

2. He Yanxi: "The best strategy is, through overall planning and vital configuration, to cause the enemy to submit together with his country."

3. In antiquity, an army was said to have 12,500 men, a regiment 500 men, a company 100, and a squad 5. During the Warring States period, the number of men in the various divisions of an army was different for each country.

4. This is, of course, an idealistic desideratum. In an actual war setting, where one is under attack by an aggressive enemy, such an approach to war would be both simplistic and impractical, as well as potentially fatal. In this regard, the defensive strategies described elsewhere in the *Sun Zi* must be considered of greater practicality and effectiveness than the suggestion that not fighting at all is the best policy.

5. Both of these were covered with heavy leather and were intended for the purpose of enabling groups of men to approach the base of the city wall, filling in the ditch in front of it as they went forward.

6. It is precisely this type of approach that is the subject of *Mo Zi*, chap. 63.

7. The phrase "attack by stratagem" is a variant translation of the same expression (*mou gong*) that is rendered in the title of this chapter as "planning for the attack."

8. With the clear understanding that all of the tactics of artifice, deception, and so forth that are advocated elsewhere in the *Sun Zi* will be employed.

9. In Zhou times, the armies were divided into three parts: the left, right, and center, or the upper, center, and lower. Later, "triple army" or "tripartite army" became a conventional designation for the army of a kingdom.

10. This is undoubtedly the best-known saying in the *Sun Zi*. It reminds one of the famous sixth-c. Greek maxim *Gnothi se auton* ("Know thyself") attributed to Solon of Athens (ca. 640–ca. 558 BC) and inscribed in gold letters over the portico to the temple of the Sun god Apollo's Oracle at Delphi, except that the version in *Sun Zi* is expanded from self-introspection to encompass extrospection.

Mao Zedong (1893–1976), the chairman of the Communist Party of the People's Republic of China, was particularly fond of this maxim from the *Sun Zi*. In his "Zhongguo geming zhanzheng de zhanlüe wenti" (Problems of strategy in China's revolutionary war), written in December 1936, he stated:

There is a saying in the book of Master Sun Wu, the great military scientist of ancient China: "He who knows his opponent and knows himself will not be imperiled in a hundred battles." This encompasses both the stage of learning and the stage of application, both knowing the laws of the development of objective reality and deciding on our own action in accordance with these laws in order to overcome the enemy before us. We should not take this saying lightly.

(near the end of chap. 1, "How to Study War")

Again, in "Lun changjiu zhan" (On protracted war), written in May 1938, he showed his extraordinary fondness for this aphorism from the *Sun Zi*:

But war is not something mysterious; it is an inevitable activity in the world. Consequently, Master Sun's rule, "If you know your opponent and know yourself, in a hundred battles you will never be imperiled," is, after all, scientific truth.

4. Positioning

1. Du Mu: "If I cannot detect any vincible formations of the enemy, then I should conceal my own formations as preparation for invincibility so as to defend myself. When the enemy reveals a vincible formation, then I should go out and attack him."

2. The received text seems to make perfectly good sense, yet the Yinque Shan manuscript offers a strikingly different wording: "If we adopt a defensive posture, we shall have more than enough; if we launch an attack, we shall not have enough." Surprisingly, this rather mystifying reading of the Yinque Shan bamboo manuscript finds confirmation in a passage from the *Han shu* (History of the Han), "Biography of Zhao Chongguo": "I have heard [N.B.] a method of war [*bingfa*] which states, 'He who does not have enough to launch an attack will have more than enough to adopt a defensive posture.'" It would appear that the original formulation (in all likelihood orally circulated) was more or less as recorded in the "Biography of Zhao Chongguo," that it became partially garbled when written down in the Yinque Shan manuscript, causing some later editor to correct the text. This correction would have occurred by the time of Cao Cao, and quite likely may have been made by Cao Cao himself, whose commentary comports with it: "The reason I adopt a defensive posture is that my strength is inadequate; the reason I launch an attack is that my strength is more than adequate."

3. Literally, "the good of the good"—the *summum bonum*. The same expression occurs in the next sentence.

4. The whole world; the empire.

5. A metaphor for something extremely light in weight.

6. The Yinque Shan manuscript and other texts of its filiation add before these two clauses, "do not [necessitate] spectacular victories," which is somewhat tautological.

7. Similar sentiments are expressed in the "Gong quan" (Tactical balance of power in attacks) chapter of the *Wei Liao Zi* (Master Wei Liao), another work of military strategy from the pre-Han period: "If one will not necessarily be victorious in war, one should not speak of battle. If one will not necessarily topple his opponent's walled city in an attack, one should not speak of attack." In both the *Sun Zi* and the *Wei Liao Zi*, the authors emphasize not leaving victory to chance.

8. The way of enlightened rulership, i.e., making the people and the ruler unified. The "way" referred to here is not the cosmological or transcendental Tao of many other Warring States schools of thought, but a more practical, goal-oriented regimen and ethos. It is spelled out more clearly in the "Ba zhen" (Eight formations) chapter of the *Sun Bin*: "He who knows the way: above, knows the way (nature) of heaven, below, knows the principles of earth, within, captures the mind of the people, without, knows the circumstances of the enemy. As for formations, he knows the parameters of the eight formations. When he sees victory, he does battle; when he does not see it, he remains still."

9. Referring to the length of earth or land, i.e., distance.

10. Referring to the size or capacity of resources.

11. The number of troops.

12. The forces or strength of oneself and one's enemy.

13. The text literally says simply "victory," but we are to understand this as "victory and defeat"; in other words, "[judging the chances for] victory [or defeat]."

14. The terms for the ancient measures of weight referred to in the text are *yi* and *zhu*. An *yi* consisted of twenty-four (or twenty) *liang* ("ounces"), and a *liang* was made up of twenty-four *zhu*. Thus, an *yi* was 576 (or 480) times heavier than a *zhu*. The metaphor is employed to show the overwhelming disparity between the advantages and disadvantages of the victor and the vanquished in a war.

15. The unit of length referred to in the text is *ren*, which is composed of eight *chi* ("foot"). Hence, we may think of it as roughly equivalent to a fathom, which comprises six feet.

16. It is somewhat odd that the last substantive word of this chapter is identical with the title, but that the topic it specifies, positioning, is not systematically addressed within the present chapter itself. For that we shall have to wait for later chapters (including the next), where it is discussed in detail.

5. Configuration

1. Wang Xi: "He who is skilled in battle can rely on configuration to achieve victory."
2. "Division" refers to dispensing tasks and responsibilities; "enumeration" signifies fixing the amounts of personnel for various units.
3. The implications of *xing* ("shape, form") and *ming* ("term, name") in this passage are much debated. In a note, Cao Cao declared, "Flags and banners are *xing*, gongs and drums are *ming*," and many later commentators have followed him in this interpretation. However, in the previous chapter, *xing* implies "positioning," and later in this chapter it is used with the meaning of "form," whereas *ming* is left hanging without further clarification. Hence, it is safest to render *xingming* more literally here.
4. The pair *qizheng* occurs four times in this chapter and nowhere else in *Sun Zi*. At the beginning of the next section, *zheng* and *qi* also occur in two closely parallel, juxtaposed phrases, and *qi* occurs once by itself in the same section as well. The tightly linked pair of technical terms, *qi* and *zheng*, are to be found only in this part of the text. In contrast, the last chapter of the Yinque Shan *Sun Bin* is entirely devoted to the bipolar concept of *qizheng*.

   Although *qizheng* is one of the most vital concepts in both *Sun Zi* and *Sun Bin*, and indeed in virtually all subsequent military thinking in China, it is fraught with fundamental problems that pose a severe challenge for modern interpreters. Among these are the precise semantic content of its two components and even the correct pronunciation of the first syllable, some of which questions are addressed at greater length in the list of "Key Terms."

5. The ancient Chinese scale was pentatonic.
6. The ancient Chinese palette consisted of cyan, red, yellow, white, and black.
7. The basic flavors were sweet, sour, bitter, hot, and salty.
8. For the antecedents and significance of the crossbow, see the introduction.
9. See n. 2, above.
10. Parts of this passage are extraordinarily terse and have required considerable amplification for the sake of intelligibility. He Yanxi: "By shifting position and changing configuration, one can tempt the enemy into making a move. Confused in battle and falling for my trap, the enemy will come forth, and I will have the strength to control him."
11. Some editions have *zu* ("soldiers, troops"), but those which have *ben* ("basis," i.e., "main/heavy [forces]") seem to make better sense here.
12. The tautological nature of the last clause (which may more literally be translated simply as "is configuration") is difficult to disguise. Its function, however, is identical to the last clause of the previous chapter, viz., as a closing recapitulation.

6. Emptiness and Solidity

1. Du You: "Go where he must rush to, attack where he must rescue. If you can defend the vital passes, the enemy will not be able to get through. Therefore, Master Wang says, 'If one cat is posted at the entrance to a hole, ten thousand mice won't dare to come out. If one tiger is stationed at a stream, ten thousand deer will not dare to cross.' This speaks to having the upper hand when defending."
2. The Yinque Shan manuscript and several later editions read this sentence as, "Appear where he [i.e., the enemy] must rush to."
3. Yue (Viet) was the chief rival of Wu, for whom Master Sun is supposed to have served as adviser.
4. This is an example of a nested quotation in which the fictive Master Sun is quoting an unspecified source of military wisdom.

5. The last fourteen words of the English sentence ("me . . . place") have been added for clarification.

6. Referring to segments of the enemy's perimeter.

7. Also called "five elements," "five forces," "five powers," "five agents," and so forth, they are metal, wood, water, fire, and earth. The five phases were considered to be the fundamental constituents of all the phenomena in the universe and correlated with the senses, directions, seasons, colors, flavors, smells, numbers, organs of the body, ad infinitum. It was further held that wood gave birth to fire, fire gave birth to earth, earth gave birth to metal, metal gave birth to water, and water gave birth to wood. Conversely, it was held that metal overcame wood, wood overcame earth, earth overcame water, water overcame fire, and fire overcame metal. Both of these cycles were conceived of as continuous, and thus having neither beginning nor end. The parallels with the correlative functioning of the four elements (*stoicheia*, viz., fire, earth, water, air) of Greek cosmology (though Aristotle had a five-element theory that accounted for quintessence) and the four elements of Indian metaphysics (or five [ether, air, fire, water, earth], the *pañca mahābhūtas*), all of which were elaborated during the second half of the first millennium, are obvious.

8. The emphasis in this passage on there being no constancy in warfare is reminiscent of the first chapter of the *Tao te ching/Dao de jing*:

The ways that can be walked are not the constant way;
The names that can be named are not the constant name.

7. The Struggle of Armies

1. Rendered more strictly, according to the original grammar, "This is one who knows the planning of how to make the circuitous straight." See also n. 3 below.

2. This passage is clearly related to the following passage in the *Shi ji* 65 biography of Sun Bin, which is identified there as deriving from a *bingfa* ("military methods"): "If one travels a hundred tricents to

rush after advantage, the general of his upper army will fall. If one travels fifty tricents to rush after advantage, [only] half his army will reach their destination." See the translation of Sun Bin's biography in the introduction.

3. Cf. n. 1; see also the discussion of this sentence in the introduction under "Stylistics and Statistics."

4. Title of an old military manual that has been lost. The fact that this chapter quotes from such a text leads one to believe that much else in the *Sun Zi* was borrowed from other sources and was not simply a record of what "Master Sun said" (as claimed at the beginning of each chapter). It is interesting to observe that, in the Yinque Shan manuscript, the quotation beginning "In the *Army Administration* it says, 'In battle,'" is preceded by the false illative conjunction *shi gu* ("for this reason").

5. More literally, "heart-mind" (*xin*). This maxim may be compared with *Lunyu* (Analects) 9.26: "The Master said, 'The three armies can be robbed of their commander, but the common man cannot be robbed of his will.'" It is also reminiscent of a quotation from a lost text called *Jun zhi* (Treatise on the army) in the *Zuo zhuan* (Chronicle of Zuo), under the twelfth year of Duke Xuan: "'By rushing in front of one's opponent, one may rob him of his resolve.'"

6. The falling off of an army's spirit is described here as occurring in the course of a day, but this is only a metaphor for a process that takes place over time. It should not be taken too literally as implying that this process can only occur in the course of a single day.

7. This clause of the translation has been much amplified from "Confront the distant with the nearby."

8. This refers, of course, to the units of the enemy army.

9. This affirmative injunction, which is clearly out of place in the midst of so many unremittingly negative injunctions, is more naturally expressed in the Yinque Shan manuscript of the *Sun Zi*: "leave [*yi*] an opening for an army that is surrounded." Here in the clumsily worded received text, one might choose to restore "leave" (*yi*), which has been replaced by "[it is] necessary [to]" (*bi*). Even with the received text, however, we can—with some effort—render the

sentence as follows: "[it is] necessary [to leave] an opening for an army that is surrounded" (this is the basis for the translation given here). Still, one wonders what possessed the author of this section to insert a single affirmative injunction in the midst of seven negative injunctions.

He Yanxi: "When Taizu of the Wei kingdom [i.e., Cao Cao] was besieging Huguan, he issued an order: 'After the city falls, bury them all!' Months passed, but yet the city did not fall. Cao Ren [his cousin] said, 'When besieging a city, one should always show an opening so that they will have a path to survival. Now, sir, you have announced that they must die, so they will go on defending themselves. Since the city walls are solid and they have much grain, an attack would result in many of our troops being wounded, and the defense will continue for a long time. To encamp under the walls of a strong city and attack rebels who are determined to die is not a good plan.' Taizu followed his advice, whereupon the city opened its gates and surrendered."

8. Nine Varieties

1. There is vast controversy among Chinese commentators over the significance of "nine" in the title. Some say that it only means "a large number of," while others contend that it literally means "nine." In either case, there have been many proposals put forward for which particular group of nine (or many) items is intended. After careful study, the reader is invited to suggest his or her own set of nine (or many) variations. A good place to begin might be to look at chapter 11, "Nine Types of Terrain," with which the present chapter shares considerable overlap and resonance.

Wang Xi: "I claim that 'nine' is simply a very large number. The method of waging war requires infinite variations."

Zhang Yu: "'Variation' is the method of not being constrained by constancy. This implies that, when one is confronting an evolving situation [i.e., something that is happening], one should follow what is appropriate and act accordingly. Whenever one is struggling with someone else for advantage, it is necessary to know the nine varieties of terrain. Therefore, this chapter comes after 'The Struggle of Armies.'"

2. The term *bian* may be more literally rendered as "transformations." However, no single translation of *bian* is suitable for this chapter, since the term is applied to widely different phenomena, including "alternatives" and "contingencies," aside from "varieties" and "transformations."

3. The Yinque Shan bamboo strip manuscripts (pp. 98–99) include a commentary on these five exclusionary ("that he does not") clauses. The commentary emphasizes and explains the specific conditions under which a general may choose not to carry out certain (viz., the first four) courses of action that he would normally be expected to take. The fifth exclusionary clause subsumes the preceding four clauses: "When the ruler's orders contravene these four contingencies, they are not to be carried out."

4. And disadvantages, of course.

5. This word is missing in the Song-period *Wu jing qi shu* (Seven military classics) and *Taiping yulan* (Imperial survey of the Great Peace [reign period]) editions of the text.

6. This probably refers to the advantages deriving from the exclusionary clauses iterated above and discussed in n. 3.

7. Since it appears so frequently at the conclusion of a passage, the injunction "they cannot be left unexamined" would appear to be a formulaic expression in the rhetoric of the period.

9. Marching the Army

1. The word used here is *xiang*, which basically means "to physiognomize," i.e., to discern the lineaments of (a person, horse, etc. [especially the face]) and determine their significance.

2. I.e., the south. The word used here is *sheng* ("living"), which Cao Cao defines as *yang* ("solar").

3. If the army is placed too close to the water before crossing, its options and maneuverability are both reduced.

4. The text literally says "right," but we may interpret this as "above" because "right" was considered superior to "left" in early Chinese writings.

Li Quan: "For advantageous usage, people all find the right to be more convenient. That is why one puts his back to it."

5. The text literally reads "in front death, behind life." The translation follows the interpretation of *Huai Nan Zi* (Master Huai Nan), "Di xing xun (An explanation of the types of terrain)": "The one that is higher is called 'life,' the one that is lower is called 'death.'"

6. Mythical founding father of the Han race and early Chinese culture.

7. A fragmentary text found together with the Yinque Shan *Sun Zi bingfa* (Yinque Shan Hanmu Zhujian Zhengli Xiaozu 1976:101) recapitulates this passage in greater detail, specifying that the Yellow Emperor "chastised the Red Emperor to the south . . . , the [Cyan] Emperor to the east . . . , the Black emperor to the north . . . , the White emperor to the west. . . . Having vanquished the Four Emperors, he possessed the whole of all-under-heaven."

8. There are clear correspondences (e.g., numerous terms beginning with *tian* ["heaven, sky"]) between this passage and *Sun Bin* 8, which deals with different types of terrain.

9. This observation is uncannily reminiscent of *Macbeth,* act 5, scene 5:

> MESSENGER: As I did stand my watch upon the hill,
> I look'd toward Birnam, and anon, methought,
> The wood began to move.
> MACBETH: Liar and slave!
> MESSENGER: Let me endure your wrath, if 't be not so:
> Within this three mile may you see it coming;
> I say, a moving grove.
> MACBETH: If thou speak'st false
> Upon the next tree shalt thou hang alive,
> Till famine cling thee: if thy speech be sooth,
> I care not if thou dost for me as much

I pull in resolution, and begin
To doubt the equivocation of the fiend
That lies like truth: "Fear not, till Birnam wood
Do come to Dunsinane": and now a wood
Comes toward Dunsinane. Arm, arm, and out!

10. Following the commentary of Cao Cao: "When the enemy spreads his flanks wide, he [intends] to come and overwhelm me" (literally, "cover me up").

11. The term *liao* implies that one gains information about his opponent, analyzes the intelligence he has gained, and then makes an informed judgment concerning how to deal with his opponent.

12. This is *wen,* the opposite of *wu* ("martial, military").

10. Terrain Types

1. More literally, this might be rendered as "Ground Forms," but see "Principles of Translation," point 3. Cf. the beginning section of chap. 8.

2. This amounts to 2.4 percent of the total number of characters in the chapter, an extremely high frequency for a verb. The author is clearly trying to make a point about the importance of awareness.

3. Li Quan: "If he cares for them like this, he will receive their utmost exertion. Therefore, the viscount of Chu had but to speak one word and all the soldiers of the triple army felt as though they were wrapped in silk floss." This is based on *Zuo zhuan,* the twelfth year of Duke Xuan, which tells how the viscount of Chu comforted his men during a bitterly cold winter campaign. The mere words of encouragement and solace he offered his men warmed them as if they were wearing clothing padded with silk floss.

Du Mu: "During the Warring States period when Wu Qi was serving as general, he wore the same clothing and ate the same food as the lowest soldiers. When he lay down he did not spread a mat; on the march, he did not ride in a chariot or mount a horse. His rations were the same meager fare as those of everyone else; and he shared in the toil and pain with the troops. Once when a soldier was suffering from an abscess, Wu Qi sucked out the pus. When the soldier's mother heard this, she cried. Somebody asked her, 'Your son is a soldier, yet the general sucked the pus out of his abscess. Why are you crying?' The mother replied, 'In a bygone year, Lord Wu sucked the pus out of his father's abscess, and he barely had a chance to turn on his heels before dying at the hands of the enemy. Now, again, Lord Wu has sucked the pus out of my son's abscess, and he is sure to die, but I know not where.'" Wu Qi was the author of another military treatise and was often paired with Sun Zi (see the introduction for further discussion).

Zhang Yu: "When the general looks upon his soldiers as his sons, the soldiers will look upon the general as their father. Now, there has never been a father in danger whose sons did not risk death to save him. Therefore, Xun Qing [Master Xun] said, 'The subject to his lord is in a position of subservience to a superior, like a son to his father or a younger brother to his older brother; they are like hands and feet that will fend for the head and the eyes.' When fine brew flows freely, the three armies will all get drunk; when a warm word is uttered, the troops will feel as though they were wearing clothes padded with silk floss. Indeed! Treating those beneath one with kindness is something that was valued by the ancients. Therefore, a *bingfa* says, 'The general must put himself at the front of an army that toils. In summer heat, he doesn't spread a sunshade; in winter cold, he doesn't wear layered clothing. In precarious places, he gets down and walks; he waits for the soldiers to dig their wells before drinking; he waits till the food for the army is cooked before eating; and he waits for the army to build ramparts before retiring to his shelter.'"

4. Cf. chap. 3 n. 10. The exact same formulation (*zhi bi zhi ji* ["know the other, know yourself"]) is also found in *Lü shi chunqiu* 16.6: "Therefore, in all cases of battle, it is necessary to be thoroughly familiar [with the situation] and completely prepared [for any eventuality]. If you know your opponent and know yourself, only then will you be successful." Since this is also in the context of war, it clearly indicates that the expression "Know your opponent and know yourself" was

part of a widely circulating body of aphorisms available to various compilers of texts. It is also worth noting that Lü Buwei, the compiler of the *Lü shi chunqiu,* precedes the sentence in which this aphorism occurs with both a false illative (*gu*) and an adverb of generality (*fan*), which occurs frequently in the *Sun Zi.*

5. These are not merely the cosmological concepts common to early Chinese thought but refer even more explicitly to natural conditions (heaven) and the topographical forms (earth) that are discussed so extensively in this and other chapters of the *Sun Zi.*

11. Nine Types of Terrain

1. Compare with the beginning of chap. 8.
2. So called because the feudal lords do not send their troops to serve under the coordinated command of the leading general of the state to which they owe fealty. Instead, the feudal lords retain control of their troops, even though they may be fighting for the cause of a king to whom they owe allegiance.
3. In the sense that it has thoroughfares linking the feudal lords with each other and the enemy as well as to the central state to which they are subordinate.
4. The verb for "march" (*xing*) is missing in some editions.
5. More literally, "[if it is] dispersed terrain, then [I do] not battle." The same structure applies to the following eight sentences, a total of nine, as indicated by the chapter title.
6. Jia Lin: "If one fights with all one's might, one may live; if one protects one's corner, one will die."
7. It is not surprising that this awkward locution is missing in some editions.
8. Meng: "By engaging in multiple subterfuges—going toward the east but appearing in the west, attacking in the south but luring him toward the north—one causes one's enemy to be crazed and confused, such that he is unable to regroup."
9. This could be a position, a general, or anything else that is of great importance to the enemy forces and energizes them.

10. It is not clear either who the questioner is or who the respondent is, but we may presume that the latter is the fictive Master Sun, who is the supposed font of military wisdom in the book that goes by his name. Although there are two fragmentary texts among the Yinque Shan manuscripts that consist of questions put by the king of Wu and answered by Master Sun, it is obviously not appropriate for the king to preface his questions by saying, "[I] make bold to ask," which is the rhetoric of someone in a subservient position. It is more likely that the two occurrences of the question-and-answer form in this chapter are remnants of a catechetical teaching method that was lost as the body of oral lore was transformed into the written text known as the *Sun Zi bingfa*. In any event, the two occurrences of the question-and-answer form in this chapter serve only, along with its extraordinary length and other unusual features, to distinguish it further from all of the rest of the chapters in the book.

11. Invading.

12. The one who is invaded.

13. Zhuan Zhu was a steely, suicidal assassin of the state of Wu during the Spring and Autumn period, and Cao Gui (or Cao Mo) was a brave warrior from Lu, also from the Spring and Autumn period. The fact that the supposed author of the *Sun Zi*, Sun Wu, invokes two legendary figures from around the same time when he is alleged to have lived casts doubt on the historicity of the man and a Spring and Autumn date for his text. Rather, the perspective here is of someone writing in the Warring States or later time and looking back to the Spring and Autumn period.

14. Following the Yinque Shan manuscript, rather than the received text, which has Mt. Chang, the latter reflecting a taboo on the use of the character for Heng because it was the personal name (Liu Heng) of the Western Han emperor Wen Di (r. 179–157 B.C.). The name of the mountain, which is located south of modern Hunyuan in Shanxi Province, was changed back to Heng during the reign of Wu Di (r. 561–578 AD) of the Northern Zhou period. Mt. Heng is the northernmost of the five sacred marchmounts.

15. The one-sentence definition of Shuairan and the extended description of it that follows read like a commentary that has worked its way into the text.

16. See n. 10 above. Here, it is not clear how far the answer extends, with some scholars holding that it ends with the simple "Yes."

17. The first ten words of the English translation ("it . . . where") have been added for purposes of clarification.

18. The word used here is *yu* ("[make] ignorant, stupid"). This is identical with the so-called *yumin zhengce* ("policy of making the people ignorant") of the *Tao te ching/Dao de jing*:

> The ancients who practiced the Way
>   Did not enlighten the people with it;
> They used it, rather, to stupefy them.
>   (chap. 65)

> The sage, in ruling,
>   hollows their hearts,
>   stuffs their stomachs,
>   weakens their wills,
>   builds up their bones.
>   (chap. 3)

19. Some commentators maintain that this refers to knowledge of the general's plans, others, that it signifies broader or more rarefied types of knowledge.

20. Here it is clearer that the general is being advised not to make the people privy to his planning and execution.

21. Again, the idea is that of putting one's men in a position from which they cannot withdraw but can only go forward.

22. The image is that of an arrow or bolt flying forward with tremendous velocity.

23. A standard expression (usually worded as "destroy cauldrons [and] sink boats"). This sentence is actually missing from some editions of the *Sun Zi*.

24. Du You: "By burning one's baggage, throwing away one's provisions, filling up one's wells, and leveling one's stoves, one shows one's determination to fight to the death."

25. This and the following few sentences, all of which occur at least once elsewhere in the *Sun Zi*, constitute a good example of the reuse of materials that must have been in broad circulation and their occasionally poor integration in written texts.

26. According to Cao Cao, this is merely another way to refer to the nine varieties of terrain discussed several times elsewhere in the text.

27. Literally, "dead."

28. See the last section of chap. 1.

29. Jia Lin: "Follow the enemy's plans in order to determine the affairs of a battle. Victory is the only thing that matters. One should not stick to hard-and-fast guidelines."

12. Incendiary Attack

1. The most famous example of the use of fire against men in Chinese history occurred during the Three Kingdoms period in the year 208 and involved the distinguished early commentator on the *Sun Zi,* Cao Cao. This is the celebrated Battle of Red Cliff (Chi Bi, located at the southern edge of modern Hubei Province, northwest of Puqi, between Honghu and Jiayu). Cao Cao (of the Wei kingdom in the north) was leading a large army of several tens of thousands of men to cross the Yangtze River southward, while his opponents, Sun Quan (of the Wu kingdom in the southeast) and Liu Bei (of the Shu Han kingdom in the southwest) had joined forces to resist him. Sun Quan's adviser and lieutenant Zhou Yu (now commander in chief) led an army of 30,000 men to do battle with Cao Cao's army at Red Cliff.

As the two armies faced each other on either side of the river, Zhou Yu's divisional subaltern Huang Gai proposed, "The enemy has more men than we do, so it will be hard to hold out against him for long. Cao Cao's boats for crossing the river are joined closely together, so it will be possible to set fire to them and burn his army."

Thereupon, Zhou Yu commanded Huang Gai to send a letter to Cao Cao declaring that he (Zhou Yu) was willing to surrender. This was, however, merely a ruse intended to buy time for Zhou Yu and Huang Gai to carry out the next stage of their plans.

It just so happened that there was a strong southeast wind blowing at this moment. Huang Gai organized a flotilla of boats filled with firewood and oil, and had them sail toward Cao Cao's massed boats. When Huang Gai's boats were less than two tricents away from Cao Cao's army, they were simultaneously all set on fire, and continued to race with the wind toward Cao Cao's fleet. The conflagration that ensued destroyed all of Cao Cao's boats and spread to his encampment on shore, engulfing it in flames. Thereupon, Zhou Yu launched a swift attack on Cao Cao's remaining troops, inflicting upon them a tremendous defeat.

The Battle of Red Cliff has been endlessly recounted in literature (poetry, drama, and fiction), and is one of the best known war stories in Chinese history.

2. Cao Cao was also involved in a memorable instance of using fire against equipment wagons and carts, but in this case he was the one who employed it effectively against his enemy. This occurred in the year 200 A.D., when Cao Cao's forces confronted the army of Yuan Shao (who had rebelled against Cao Cao) at Guan Du ("Official Ferry"). Upon learning that Yuan Shao's army was being supplied by a convoy of ten thousand poorly protected wagons and carts, Cao Cao immediately led a contingent of five thousand select troops, who rushed to the convoy. Cao Cao's men set fire to the convoy, destroying a vast amount of grain, fodder, and other essential supplies. When news of this horrendous loss reached Yuan Shao's army at Guan Du, panic ensued, enabling Cao Cao to lead his army in attack and to gain a major victory over his rival.

Chen Hao: "If the enemy has goods that he cherishes, one may attack him (with fire). When he comes out to save them, then I have used fire to divide his configuration. All the more, when he is distraught (over the loss of his goods), one can naturally destroy his armies and kill his general."

3. There were a total of twenty-eight of these constellations into which the celestial sphere was divided by ancient Chinese astronomers. They are comparable to the twenty-seven or twenty-eight Indian *nakṣatra*s (see Joseph Needham, in *Science and Civilisation in China*, vol. 3, pp. 252–59 [1959], who asserts that their common origin can hardly be doubted; see also Pingree 1963 for the commonalty of astronomical wisdom among Greeks, Babylonians, Indians, Iranians, and Chinese). There is no scientific evidence that the winds consistently blow more strongly during the four categories of days mentioned here than during days belonging to any of the other twenty-four lunar lodges.

4. The *Sun Zi* might well have included another, separate chapter on hydraulic attacks, since this form of warfare was also highly developed during the late Warring States and later periods for undermining city walls, flooding enemy camps, and so on. During World War II, Generalissimo Chiang Kai-shek breached the dikes of the Yellow River (which actually flows above the flood plain through much of its middle and lower valley), inundating vast tracts of land in his desperate attempt to slow the advance of Japanese forces.

5. The commentators are in disarray over the meaning of this passage, with some asserting that it has to do with not being dilatory in rewarding those who are meritorious in victory and others claiming that it is concerned with the swift consolidation of one's gains.

6. Mei Yaochen: "The anger of a moment can easily turn to joy; the irritation of a moment can easily turn to happiness. But a nation that is lost and an army that has perished cannot be restored."

13. Using Spies

1. A note by Cao Cao explains, "Of old, the people were organized into neighborhoods of eight households. If a man from one of those households went off to join the army, the seven other households would have to support him. Hence, the text says that when an army of a hundred thousand is raised, 700,000 households do not devote themselves to plowing and tending the crops."

2. In the view of the author of this chapter, such persons are said to be inhumane because their stinginess prevents them from seeing the reasonableness of paying for espionage. Consequently, they ignore the best interests of the state and the welfare of the people, both of which would be improved by quality espionage.

3. This refers chiefly to intelligence concerning the enemy's actions and intentions.

4. The commentators hold diverse opinions about the referents of "symbols" and "things." They range from "analogies to past affairs" to the reading of omens and the interpretation of divination.

5. Some editions of the *Sun Zi* give just "enemy" here. The spies who spread false rumors risk death because they are usually executed as soon as the enemy finds out he has been duped.

6. Chen Hao: "If a matter pertaining to espionage has not yet been launched and someone comes to report about it, then the spy who is involved and the person who reported it should both be put to death to seal their mouths and prevent the enemy from learning of it."

7. Better known as the Shang Dynasty (ca. 1650–1045 B.C.).

8. Yi Zhi (better known as Yi Yin) and Lü Ya (better known as Jiang Ziya or Jiang Tai Gong ["Grand Duke Jiang"]) are among the few officials in Chinese history who are honored for having shifted their allegiance to a newly risen dynasty. Usually it is considered a mark of loyalty for an official to refuse to serve a conqueror. In the case of Yi Yin and Jiang Ziya, they were considered to be perceptive and righteous because they recognized the evil of the late Xia and the late Shang, respectively, and helped to bring them to a timely end.

Appendix. The Pseudo-Biography of Sun Wu

1. A northeastern state located in what is now the province of Shandong.

2. Soldierly methods; Methods of war; Art of war; Strategy.

3. Variant Helü; r. 514–496 B.C. Judging from the graphic variants of the Wu king's name and the lack of a Sinitic surname, it would appear that he was of non-Sinitic descent.

4. A southeastern state located in what is now modern Jiangsu Province.

5. This refers to the *Sun Zi bingfa,* thirteen being the number of chapters in the extant version of the text. In the bibliographical "Yiwen zhi" (Treatise on literary arts) of the *Han shu* (History of the [Western] Han Dynasty), s. 30, *Sun Zi bingfa* is listed as having eighty-two chapters and nine scrolls of illustrations. This is somewhat puzzling, because we here have the historian, Sima Qian, indicating in the early first century B.C. that the *Sun Zi* had thirteen chapters, and this exactly matches the number of chapters of both the received text and the recently discovered bamboo manuscripts of the *Sun Zi.* The fact that the *Han shu* is a work of the first century A.D., albeit incorporating materials from the first century B.C. (including major components of its bibliographical treatise devised by Liu Xiang [ca. 77–8 B.C.] and his son Liu Xin [d. 23 A.D.]), means that there must have been a quite different recension of the *Sun Zi* in circulation at that time, after the stabilization of the received text by the early second c. B.C., two centuries earlier.

It is quite possible, however, that the *Sun Zi bingfa* listed in the bibliographical treatise of the *Han shu* does not refer to the work attributed to Sun Wu, but to another work altogether. As a matter of fact, the entry in the bibliographical entry in the *Han shu* designates the work in question as *Wu Sun Zi bingfa* (Soldierly methods of Master Sun of the state of Wu). This might conceivably refer to the legendary Sun Wu (Sun the Martial) who allegedly composed the thirteen-chapter *Sun Zi bingfa,* because he was alleged to have a connection with the state of Wu, but then why would he be credited with an eighty-two-chapter work in the *Han shu*? Furthermore, it was not until the early Tang period that the commentator Yan Shigu (579–645) added a note to the entry in the *Han Shu* identifying this Sun Zi as Sun Wu (Sun the Martial).

It is conceivable that the eighty-two-chapter text mentioned in the *Han shu* is actually a reference to the *Sun Bin bingfa.* In his *Shi ji* biography, which is much more detailed, substantial, and historically plausible than that of the legendary Sun Wu that precedes it, Sun Bin is also referred to as Sun Zi (Master Sun). What is more, with the chapters of the *Sun Bin bingfa* recovered from Yinque Shan, including both the sixteen main chapters plus the fifteen supplemental chapters, together with three other chapters recovered from later commentarial, historical, and encyclopedic sources (Lau and Ames 2003), we know of a total of thirty-four chapters associated with Sun Bin. This large number of Sun Bin chapters suggests the possibility that there may well have been others that still existed at the end of the Han Dynasty. On the contrary, it is clear that the number of chapters associated with the legendary Sun Wu was already stabilized at thirteen at least a century before the time when the Yinque Shan manuscripts were entombed.

6. The text literally says that "the three orders were stated five times." This was customary in old military drills to ensure that there would be absolutely no misunderstanding or mistake on the part of the recruits.

7. Master Sun had obviously also instructed his charges on the drum signals that were used to indicate different directions, but this is not mentioned in the text.

8. A direct quotation from the eighth chapter of the received text of the *Sun Zi*.

9. Most likely decapitated with the battle-ax, though the verb used in the text (*zhan*) literally means "cut in two at the waist."

10. This directly contradicts Master Sun's assertion above that he had already been commanded by the king to be a general in the king's army. Apparently, however, that was only a temporary appointment for conducting the trial drills with the two companies of palace women.

11. A large southern state that covered modern Hubei and Hunan provinces.

12. This occurred in 506 B.C. The complex circumstances surrounding Wu's capture of Ying have been thoroughly studied by modern scholars writing in English. See Rudolph (1942; 1962) and Johnson (1980; 1981). Mair (1983:123–65, 262–305) presents a popular medieval account of the conflict between Wu and Chu.

13. An important northern state that stretched across much of the Central Plains in what is now modern Shanxi Province.

14. The last paragraph of this "biography" of Sun Wu is like a capsule summary of events recounted in *Shi ji,* s. 66, "The Biography of Wu Zixu" (Nienhauser 1994: 49–62).

N.B.: Many early Chinese texts (e.g., Guan Zi, Huainan Zi, Han Fei Zi, Xun Zi, Lü shi chunqiu, Chunqiu Zuozhuan, etc.) have been consulted in The ICS Ancient Chinese Texts Concordance Series compiled by the Institute for Chinese Studies of the Chinese University of Hong Kong, but these have not been entered separately in the bibliography. See, however, Liu Dianjue (D. C. Lau) for the volume on the militarists. Nor are the translations of the Chinese classics by James Legge, which are available in numerous reprints, listed individually in the bibliography. The twenty-four standard dynastic histories are cited according to the editions published by Zhonghua Shuju from 1962 through 1975.

Aineias the Tactician. 1990 [ca. 350 B.C.] *How to Survive Under Siege.* Trans., intro., and comm., David Whitehead. Oxford: Clarendon.

Amano Shizuo, trans. and annot. 1972. *Sonshi, Goshi* (Sun Zi, Wu Zi). Shinshaku kanbun taikei (New series of translations from Chinese literature), 36. Tokyo: Meiji shoin.

Ames, Roger T., trans., intro., and comm. 1993. *Sun-tzu: The Art of Warfare.* New York: Ballantine.

Amiot, Joseph Marie, trans. 1772. *Art militaire des Chinois, ou Receuil d'anciens traités sur la guerre, composés avant l'ère chrétienne, par différents généraux chinois. Ouvrages sur lesquels les aspirants aux grades militaries sont obligés de subir des examens. On y a joint dix préceptes addressés aux troupes par l'empereur Yong-tcheng, père de l'empereur régnant. Et des planches gravées pour l'intelligence des exercices, des évolutions, des habillements, des armes & des instruments militaries des Chinois. Tr. en françois, par le P. Amiot, rev. & pub. Par M. Geguignes.* Paris: Didot l'ainé. Rpt. as vol. 7 in Joseph Marie Amiot, François Bourgeois, Pierre Martial Cibot, Aloys Kao, Aloys de Poirot, Charles Batteux, Bréquigny, M. de, Antoine Gaubil, Antoine Isaac Silvestre de Sacy, Baron. *Mémoires concernant l'histoire, les sciences, les arts, les moeurs, les usages, &c. des Chinois: par les missionaries de Pékin.* Paris: Nyon, 1776–1814.

An Zhimin. 1993. "Shilun Zhongguo de zaoqi tongqi" (A tentative discussion on China's early copper/bronze implements). *Kaogu* (Archeology), 12:1110–19.

Anthony, David W. 2007. *The Horse, the Wheel, and Language.* Princeton, N.J.: Princeton University Press.

Asano Yuichi, trans. and annot. 1986. *Sonshi.* Tokyo: Kodansha.

Bagley, Robert. 1999. "Shang Archaeology." In *The Cambridge History of Ancient China: From the Origins of Civilization to 221 B.C.,* ed. Michael Loewe and Edward L. Shaughnessy, 124–231. Cambridge: Cambridge University Press.

Balmforth, Edmund Elliott. 1979. "A Chinese Military Strategist of the Warring States, Sun Pin." 2 vols. Ph.D. diss., Rutgers University.

Boodberg, Peter A. 1930. "The Art of War in Ancient China: A Study Based Upon the *Dialogues of Li, Duke of Wei.*" Ph.D. diss., University of California at Berkeley.

Boorman, Scott A. 1969. *The Protracted Game: A Wei-ch'i Interpretation of Maoist Revolutionary Strategy.* New York: Oxford University Press.

Brooks, E. Bruce. 1994. Review Article: "The Present State and Future Prospects of Pre-Hàn Text Studies." *Sino-Platonic Papers* 46 (July): 1–74

Brooks, E. Bruce, and A. Taeko Brooks, trans. and comm. 1976. *Chinese Character Frequency Lists.* Northampton, Mass.: SinFac Minor.

——. 1998. *The Original Analects: Sayings of Confucius and His Successors.* New York: Columbia University Press.

Calthrop, E[verard] F[erguson], trans. 1905. *Sonshi: The Chinese Military Classic.* Tokyo: Sanseido, 1905. Republished as *The Book of War: The Military Classic of the Far East.* London: J. Murray.

Carman, W. Y. 2004 [1955]. *A History of Firearms: From Earliest Times to 1914.* Mineola, N.Y.: Dover. Originally published by Routledge & Kegan Paul.

Clausewitz, Carl von. 1911. *On War.* Trans. J. J. Graham. 3 vols. London: Kegan Paul, Trench, Trübner.

——. 1976. *On War.* Trans. Michael Howard and Peter Paret. Princeton, N.J.: Princeton University Press.

——. 2004. *Principles of War.* Trans., ed., and intro. Hans W. Gatzke. Mineola, N.Y.: Dover. Originally published by The Military Service Publishing Company, Harrisburg, Penn., 1942.

Cowley, Robert, and Geoffrey Parker, eds. 1996. *The Reader's Companion to Military History.* Boston: Houghton.

Creel, H. G. 1965. "The Role of the Horse in Chinese History." *American Historical Review* 70, no. 3 (April): 647–72.

Deng Zezong. 1986. *Sun Bin bingfa zhu yi* [Sun Bin's soldierly methods, with annotations and translation]. Beijing: Jiefang Jun Chuban She.

Di Cosmo, Nicola. 1999. "The Northern Frontier in Pre-Imperial China." In *The Cambridge History of Ancient China: From the Origins of Civilization to 221 B.C.,* ed. Michael Loewe and Edward L. Shaughnessy, 885–966. Cambridge: Cambridge University Press.

Dubs, Homer H. 1947. "The Beginnings of Alchemy." *Isis* 38, no. 1–2 (November): 62–86.

Eno, Robert. 2003. "The Background of the Kong Family of Lu and the Origins of Ruism." *Early China* 28:1–41.

Fairbank, John K. 1974. "Introduction: Varieties of the Chinese Military Experience." In *Chinese Ways in Warfare,* ed. Frank A. Kierman and John K. Fairbank, 1–26. Cambridge, Mass.: Harvard University Press.

Falkenhausen, Lothar von. 1999. "The Waning of the Bronze Age: Material Culture and Social Developments, 770–481 B.C." In *The Cambridge History of Ancient China: From the Origins of Civilization to*

221 B.C., ed. Michael Loewe and Edward L. Shaughnessy, 450–544. Cambridge: Cambridge University Press.

———. 2006. *Chinese Society in the Age of Confucius, 1000–250 BC: The Archeological Evidence.* Los Angeles: Cotsen Institute of Archaeology, University of California.

Frontinus. 1969 [ca. 84–96 A.D.]. *The Stratagems and The Aqueducts of Rome.* Trans. Charles E. Bennett. Ed. Mary R. McElwain. Loeb Classical Library. Cambridge, Mass.: Harvard University Press. London: William Heinemann.

Gawlikowski, Krzysztof, and Michael Loewe. 1993. "*Sun tzu ping fa.*" In *Early Chinese Texts,* ed. Loewe, 446–55. Early China Special Monograph Series, No. 2. Berkeley: The Society for the Study of Early China and the Institute of East Asian Studies, University of California, Berkeley.

Giles, Lionel, trans. and annot. 1910. *Sun Tzù on the Art of War.* Shanghai and London: Luzac.

Goldin, Paul R. 2005a. "The *Methods of War* of Sun Wu and Sun Bin." In *Hawai'i Reader in Traditional Chinese Culture,* ed. Victor H. Mair, Nancy S. Steinhardt, and Paul R. Goldin, 113–20. Honolulu: University of Hawai'i Press.

———. 2005b. "Sima Qian, 'Letter to Ren An.'" In *Hawai'i Reader in Traditional Chinese Culture,* ed. Victor H. Mair, Nancy S. Steinhardt, and Paul R. Goldin, 178–82. Honolulu: University of Hawai'i Press.

Graham, A. C. 1993. "Mo tzu." In *Early Chinese Texts: A Bibliographic Guide,* ed. Michael Loewe, 336–41. Early China Special Monograph Series, No. 2. Berkeley: The Society for the Study of Early China and The Institute of East Asian Studies, University of California, Berkeley.

Griffith, Samuel B., trans. and comm. 1963. *Sun Tzu: The Art of War.* Foreword by B. H. Liddell Hart. London: Oxford University Press.

Henricks, Robert G., ed., trans., and annot. 2000. *Lao Tzu's* Tao Te Ching: *A Translation of the Startling New Documents Found at Guodian.* New York: Columbia University Press.

Hua Jueming, Yang Gen, and Liu Enzhu. 1960. "Zhanguo liang Han tieqi de jinxiangxue kaocha chubu baogao" (Preliminary report on a metallographic investigation of iron implements from the Warring States and two Han periods). *Kaogu xuebao* (The Chinese journal of archaeology) 1:73–88, plates 1–8.

Huang Kui. 1996. *Sun Zi bingfa* (Master Sun's military methods). Mingzhu mingjia daodu (Guides to the study of famous works and famous authors). Chengdu: Ba-Shu shushe.

Huang Zhenhua. 1992. "Xi Xia wen *Sun Zi bingfa* san jia zhu guankui: Sun Zi yanjiu zhaji zhi yi" (A glimpse at the Tangut text of *Sun Zi's Soldierly Methods* with three commentaries: First in a series of notes on studies of the *Sun Zi*). In *Xi Xia wenshi luncong, I* (Studies on the history and culture of the Tanguts, I), ed. Ningxia Wenwu Guanli Weiyuanhui Bangongshi (Office of the Administrative Committee for Cultural Relics of Ningxia Province) and Ningxia Wenhua Ting Wenwu Chu (Cultural Relics Department of the Cultural Bureau of Ningxia Province), 112–21. Yinchuan: Ningxia Renmin Chubanshe.

Hummel, Arthur W., ed. 1943. *Eminent Chinese of the Ch'ing Period (1644–1912)*. Washington, D.C.: United States Government Printing Office.

Johnson, David. 1980. "The Wu Tzu-hsü *pien-wen* and Its Sources: Parts I and II." *Harvard Journal of Asiatic Studies*, 40, no. 1 (June): 93–156; 40, no. 2 (December): 465–505.

———. 1981. "Epic and History in Early China: The Matter of Wu Tzu-hsü." *Journal of Asian Studies* 40, no. 2 (February): 255–71.

Johnston, Ian, trans., ed., intro., and annot. Forthcoming. *The Mozi*. Hong Kong: The Chinese University of Hong Kong Press; New York: Columbia University Press.

Jullien, François. 1995. *The Propensity of Things: Toward A History of Efficacy in China*. Trans. Janet Lloyd. New York: Zone Books. English version of *La propension des choses: pour une histoire de l'efficacité en Chine*. Paris: Seiul, 1992.

Kanaya Osamu, Kuraishi Takeshirō, Seki Masao, Fukunaga Mitsuji, and Murayama Yoshihiro, trans. 1973. *Rōshi, Sōshi, Resshi, Sonshi, Goshi* (Lao Zi, Zhuang Zi, Lie Zi, Sun Zi, and Wu Zi). Chugoku koten bungaku taikei (Classical Chinese literature series), 4. Tokyo: Heibonsha.

Kangle, R. P., ed., trans., and annot. 1988 [1972]. *The Kauṭilya Arthaśāstra.* 3 vols. Reprint ed. Delhi: Motilal Banarsidass.

Karlgren, Bernhard. 1972. *Grammata Serica Recensa.* Stockholm: Museum of Far Eastern Antiquities.

Keegan, John. 1993. *A History of Warfare.* London: Hutchinson; New York: Alfred A. Knopf. Pbk. rpt., New York: Vintage (Random House), 1994.

Keping, K. B., trans., comm., and annot. 1979. *Sun Tsz'i v Tangutskom Perevode.* With facsimiles of the entire woodblock-printed text, extensive grammatical analysis, dictionary, etc. Pamyatniki Pis'mennosti Vostoka, 44. Moscow: Nauka, Glavnaya Redaktsiya Vostochnoi Literatur'i.

Kierman, Frank A., Jr. 1974. "Phases and Modes of Combat in Early China." In *Chinese Ways in Warfare,* ed. Frank A. Kierman Jr. and John K. Fairbank, 27–66. Cambridge: Harvard University Press.

Kierman, Frank A., Jr., and John K. Fairbank, eds. 1974. *Chinese Ways in Warfare.* Cambridge: Harvard University Press.

Kolb, Raimund Theodor. 1991. *Die Infanterie im Alten China: Ein Beitrag zur Militärgeschichte der Vor-Zhanguo-Zeit.* Materialen zur Allgemeinen und Vergleichenden Archäologie, Band 43. Mainz: Philipp von Zabern.

Konrad, N. I., trans. and comm. 1950. *Sun'-tsz'y: Traktat o voennom iskusstve.* Moscow: Izdatelstvo Akademii Nauk. Rpt., in the translator's collected works, *Izbrannye trudy, Sinologia.* Moscow: Nauka, Glavnaya Redaktsiya Vostochnoi Literatur'i , 1978.

Kuzmina, Elena E. 2007. *The Prehistory of the Silk Road.* Philadelphia: University of Pennsylvania Press.

Lau, D. C. 1965. "Some Notes on the *Sun Tzu.*" *Bulletin of the School of Oriental and African Studies* 28, no. 2:319–35.

——. 1992. *A Concordance to the Militarists.* See Liu Dianjue.

Lau, D. C., and Roger T. Ames, trans. and intro. 2003. *Sun Bin: The Art of Warfare. A Translation of the Classic Chinese Work of Philosophy and Strategy.* Albany: State University of New York Press.

Lewis, Mark Edward. 1990. *Sanctioned Violence in Early China.* Albany: State University of New York Press.

——. 1999. "Warring States Political Philosophy." In *The Cambridge History of Ancient China: From the Origins of Civilization to 221 B.C.*, ed. Michael Loewe and Edward L. Shaughnessy, 587–650. Cambridge: Cambridge University Press.

——. 2005. "Writings on Warfare Found in Ancient Chinese Tombs." *Sino-Platonic Papers*, 158 (August): 1–15.

——. 2007. *The Early Empires: Qin and Han. History of Imperial China*, vol. 1. Cambridge, Mass.: Harvard University Press.

Li Ling. 1995. *Sun Zi guben yanjiu* (Studies on the ancient texts of the *Sun Zi*). Beijing: Beijing Daxue Chuban She.

——. 1997. *Wu Sun Zi fawei* (An exposition of the finer points of Master Sun of Wu). Beijing: Zhonghua Shuju.

——. 2006. *Sun Zi shisan pian zonghe yanjiu* (Comprehensive studies on the thirteen chapters of the *Sun Zi*). Beijing: Zhonghua Shuju.

Lin Bao, comp. 1994 [812]. *Yuanhe xingzuan* (Compilation of surnames from the primal accord reign period). Ed. Yu Xianhao and Tao Min. Annot. Cen Zhongmian. Beijing: Zhonghua Shuju.

Liu Dianjue (D. C. Lau), ed. 1992. *Bingshu si zhong: Sun Zi, Wei Liao Zi, Wu Zi, Sima fa* (English title: *A Concordance to the Militarists [Sunzi, Yuliaozi, Wuzi, Simafa]*). Xianggang Zhongwen Daxue Zhongguo Wenhua Yanjiu Suo (The Chinese University of Hong Kong, Institute of Chinese Studies). Xian-Qin, liang Han guji zhuzi suoyin congkan (The ICS ancient Chinese text concordance series). Hong Kong: Commercial Press.

Liu, James J. Y. 1967. *The Chinese Knight Errant*. London: Routledge & Kegan Paul.

Loehr, Max. 1956. *Chinese Bronze Age Weapons: The Werner Jannings Collection in the National Palace Museum*. Ann Arbor: The University of Michigan Press; London: Geoffrey Cumberlege, Oxford University Press.

Loewe, Michael. 1977. "Manuscripts Found Recently in China: A Preliminary Survey." *T'oung Pao* 63, nos. 2–3:99–136.

——, ed. 1993. *Early Chinese Texts: A Bibliographic Guide*. Early China Special Monograph Series, No. 2. Berkeley: The Society for the Study of Early China and The Institute of East Asian Studies, University of California, Berkeley.

——. 1999. "The Heritage Left to the Empires." In *The Cambridge History of Ancient China: From the Origins of Civilization to 221 B.C.*, ed. Michael Loewe and Edward L. Shaughnessy, 966–1032. Cambridge: Cambridge University Press.

Loewe, Michael, and Edward L. Shaughnessy, eds. 1999. *The Cambridge History of Ancient China: From the Origins of Civilization to 221 B.C.* Cambridge: Cambridge University Press.

Luo Zhufeng. 1986–1994. *Hanyu da cidian* (Unabridged dictionary of Sinitic). 12 vols. plus index vol. Shanghai: Hanyu Da Cidian Chubanshe.

Machiavelli, Niccolò. 2006. *The Art of War*. Mineola, New York: Dover. This is a modernized republication of *The Art of War, in Seven Books*, excerpted from *The Works of the Famous Nicholas Michiavel, Citizen and Secretary of Florence*, trans. Henry Neville, first published in 1674. The appendix is taken from *The Arte of War*, Peter Whitehorne's translation of the same work, which first appeared in 1560.

Mair, Victor H., trans. and annot. 1983. *Tun-huang Popular Narratives*. Cambridge: Cambridge University Press.

——, trans. and comm. 1990a. *Tao Te Ching: The Classic Book of Integrity and the Way*. New York: Bantam.

——. 1990b. "Old Sinitic *m^yag*, Old Persian *maguš*, and English 'Magician.'" *Early China* 15:27–47.

——. 1993. "The Linguistic and Textual Antecedents of *The Sūtra of the Wise and the Foolish*." *Sino-Platonic Papers* 38 (April): 1–95.

——, trans. and comm. 1994. *Wandering on the Way: Early Taoist Tales and Parables of Chuang Tzu*. New York: Bantam Books. Reprint, Honolulu: University of Hawai'i Press, 1998.

——. 2003. "The Horse in Late Prehistoric China: Wresting Culture and Control from the 'Barbarians.'" In *Prehistoric steppe adaptation and the horse*, ed. Marsha Levine, Colin Renfrew, and Katie Boyle, 163–87. McDonald Institute Monographs. Cambridge: McDonald Institute for Archaeological Research, University of Cambridge.

——. 2004. "The Beginnings of Sino-Indian Cultural Contact." *Journal of Asian History* 38, no. 2:81–96.

——. 2005a. "The North(west)ern Peoples and the Recurrent Origins of the 'Chinese' State." In *The Teleology of the Modern Nation-State: Japan and China*, ed. Joshua A. Fogel, 46–84, 205–17. Philadelphia: University of Pennsylvania Press.

——. 2005b. "Genes, Geography, and Glottochronology: The Tarim Basin during Late Prehistory and History." In *Proceedings of the Sixteenth Annual UCLA Indo-European Conference*, ed. Karlene Jones-Bley, Martin E. Huld, Angela Della Volpe, and Miriam Robbins Dexter, 1–46. Los Angeles, November 5–6, 2004. Journal of Indo-European Studies Monograph Series, No. 50. Washington, D.C.: Institute for the Study of Man.

——. 2007. "Horse Sacrifices and Sacred Groves Among the North(west)ern Peoples of East Asia." *Ouya xuekan* (Journal of Eurasian studies) 6:22–53.

Mallory, James P. 2006. "Indo-European Warfare." *Journal of Conflict Archaeology* 2:77–98.

Mallory, J. P., and Victor H. Mair. 2000. *The Tarim Mummies: Ancient China and the Mystery of the Earliest Peoples from the West*. New York: Thames & Hudson.

Maspero, Henri. 1978. *China in Antiquity*. Trans. Frank A. Kierman Jr. Amherst: University of Massachusetts Press. Translation of the revised edition of *La Chine antique*, published in Paris by Imprimerie Nationale in 1965 and reissued as part of the *Annales du Musée Guimet, Bibliothèque d'Études*, 71, by Presses Universitaires de France. Originally published as vol. 4 of *Histoire du Monde* by E. De Boccard in Paris, 1927.

Mayor, Adrienne. 2003. *Greek Fire, Poison Arrows, and Scorpion Bombs: Biological and Chemical Warfare in the Ancient World*. Woodstock, N.Y.: Overlook Duckworth.

Napoleon I (Bonaparte). 2004. *Napoleon's Military Maxims*. Ed. and annot. William E. Cairnes. Trans. George C. D'Aguilar. Mineola, N.Y.: Dover. Originally published by Freemantle and Co., London, in 1901, as *The Military Maxims of Napoleon*.

Needham, Joseph. 1959. With the collaboration of Wang Ling. *Science and Civilisation in China*. Volume 3: *Mathematics and the Sciences of the Heavens and the Earth*. Cambridge: Cambridge University Press.

——. 1964. *The Development of Iron and Steel Technology in China*. Second Biennial Dickinson Memorial Lecture to the Newcomen Society 1956. London: Published for the Newcomen Society by W. Heffer and Sons.

Needham, Joseph, and Robin D. S. Yates. 1994. With the collaboration of Krzysztof Gawlikowski, Edward McEwen, and Wang Ling. *Science and Civilisation in China*. Volume 5: *Chemistry and Chemical Technology*. Part 6: Military Technology: Missiles and Sieges. Cambridge: Cambridge University Press.

Nienhauser, William H., Jr., ed. 1994. *The Grand Scribe's Records*. Vol. 7. *The Memoirs of Pre-Han China*, by Ssu-ma Ch'ien. Trans. Tsui-fa Cheng, Zongli Lu, William H. Nienhauser Jr., and Robert Reynolds. With the assistance of Chiu-ming Chan. Bloomington: Indiana University Press.

Norman, Jerry, and Tsu-Lin Mei. 1976. "The Austroasiatics in Ancient South China: Some Lexical Evidence." *Monumenta Serica* (*Journal of Oriental Studies*) 32:274–301.

Oxford Latin Dictionary. Ed. P. G. W. Glare. Oxford: Clarendon, 1982.

Partington, J. R. 1960. *A History of Greek Fire and Gunpowder*. Cambridge: W. Heffer and Sons.

Petersen, Jens Østergård. 1992a. "What's in a Name? On the Sources Concerning Sun Wu." *Asia Major*, 3rd series, 5, no. 1:1–31.

——. 1992b. "On the Expressions Commonly Held to Refer to Sun Wu, the Putative Author of the *Sunzi Bingfa*." *Acta Orientalia* 53:106–21.

Pingree, David. 1963. "Astronomy and Astrology in India and Iran." *Isis* 54, no. 2 (June): 229–46.

Pratt, Fletcher. 2000 [1956]. *The Battles that Changed History*. Mineola, N.Y.: Dover.

Qi Sihe. 1939. "Sun Zi zhuzuo shidai kao" (A Study of the Date of the Writing of the *Sun Zi*). *Yanjing xuebao* (Yanjing journal) 26:175–90.

Rand, Christopher C. 1977. "The Role of Military Thought in Early Chinese Intellectual History." Ph.D. diss., Harvard University.

——. 1979. "Li Ch'üan and Chinese Military Thought." *Harvard Journal of Asiatic Studies* 39, no. 1 (June): 107–37.

——. 1979–1980. "Chinese Military Thought and Philosophical Taoism." *Monumenta Serica (Journal of Oriental Studies)* 34:171–218.

Rawson, Jessica. 1999. "Western Zhou Archaeology." In *The Cambridge History of Ancient China: From the Origins of Civilization to 221 B.C.,* ed. Michael Loewe and Edward L. Shaughnessy, 352–449. Cambridge: Cambridge University Press.

Rickett, W. Allyn, trans. and comm. 1985. *Guanzi: Political, Economic, and Philosophical Essays from Early China.* Vol. 1. Princeton, N.J.: Princeton University Press.

Rudolph, Richard Casper. 1942. "Wu Tzu-hsü, His Life and Posthumous Cult: A Critical Study of *Shih chi* 66." Ph.D. diss., University of California at Berkeley.

——. 1962. "The *Shih-chi* Biography of Wu Tzu-hsü." *Oriens Extremis* 9:106–20.

Sawyer, Ralph D., trans. and comm. 1993. *The Seven Military Classics of Ancient China.* With the collaboration of Mei-chün Sawyer. Boulder, Colo.: Westview.

——, trans. and comm. 1995. *Sun Pin: Military Methods.* With the collaboration of Mei-chün Lee Sawyer. Boulder, Colo.: Westview.

——. 2004. *Fire and Water: The Art of Incendiary and Aquatic Warfare in China.* Boulder, Colo.: Westview.

Schipper, Kristofer, and Franciscus Verellen, eds. 2004. *The Taoist Canon: A Historical Companion to the* Daozang. 3 vols. Chicago and London: University of Chicago Press.

Schuessler, Axel. 1987. *A Dictionary of Early Zhou Chinese.* Honolulu: University of Hawai'i Press.

Shahar, Meir. 2001. "Ming-Period Evidence of Shaolin Martial Practice." *Harvard Journal of Asiatic Studies* 61, no. 2 (December): 359–413.

Shandong Shehui Kexue Yuan Sun Zi Yanjiu Zhongxin (Shandong Academy of Social Sciences, Center for the Study of the *Sun Zi*) and

Shandong Sheng Huimin Xian Sun Zi Shuyuan (Shandong Province Huimin County *Sun Zi* Academy). See Xie Xianghao and Liu Shenning (1993).

Shaughnessy, Edward L. 1988. "Historical Perspectives on the Introduction of the Chariot into China." *Harvard Journal of Asiatic Studies* 48, no. 1 (June): 189–237.

———. 1989. "Western Cultural Innovations in China, 1200 B.C." *Sino-Platonic Papers* 11 (July): 1–8.

———. 1996. "Military Histories of Early China: A Review Article." *Early China* 21:159–82.

Shepherd, R., trans. 1974 [1793]. *Polyaenus's Stratagems of War.* Chicago: Ares.

Sofronov, M[ikhail] V[iktorovitsch]. 1991. "Chinese Philology and the Scripts of Central Asia." *Sino-Platonic Papers* 30:1–9.

Sun Zi xuekan (Journal of Sun Zi studies). 1992–. Includes copious bibliographies of works in Chinese.

Tang Jigen. 1993. "Zhongguo yetieshu de qiyuan wenti" (The question of the origins of Chinese iron metallurgy). *Kaogu* (Archaeology) 6:553, 556–65.

Wakeman, Charles Bunnell. 1990. "Hsi Jung (the Western Barbarians): An Annotated Translation of the Five Chapters of the T'ung Tien on the Peoples and Countries of Pre-Islamic Central Asia." Ph.D. diss., University of California at Los Angeles.

Waldron, Arthur. 1990. *The Great Wall of China: From History to Myth.* Cambridge: Cambridge University Press.

Wang Li, ed. 2000. *Wang Li gu Hanyu zidian* (Wang Li dictionary of Old Sinitic). Beijing: Zhonghua Shuju.

Wilkinson, Endymion. 2000. *Chinese History: A Manual.* Rev. and enlgd. ed. Harvard-Yenching Institute Monograph Series, 52. Cambridge, Mass.: Harvard University Asia Center. 1st ed., 1998.

Wu Jiulong, et al., ed. 1985. *Yinque Shan Hanjian shiwen* (Transcription of the Yinque Shan Han bamboo strips). Beijing: Wenwu.

———. 2000 [1990]. *Sun Zi jiaoshi* (Collation and Explanation of the *Sun Zi*). *Sun Zi bingfa* daquan xilie congshu (A collection of works to accompany the complete *Soldierly Methods of Master Sun* series). Beijing: Junshi Kexue Chuban She.

Xie Xianghao and Liu Shenning, comp. 1993. *Sun Zi jicheng* (Comprehensive collection of edited and annotated editions of the *Sun Zi*). 24 vols. Includes eighty editions plus a large bibliography. Ji'nan: Qi-Lu Shushe.

Yamai Yū, trans. 1975. *Sonshi, Goshi* (Sun Zi, Wu Zi). Zenshaku kanbun taikei (Complete translations of Chinese literature), 22. Tokyo: Shūeisha.

Yang Bing'an, ed. 1986. Sun Zi *hui jian* (Assembled notes on the *Sun Zi*). Henan [*sic*]: Zhongzhou Guji.

———, ed. 1999. *Shiyi jia zhu* Sun Zi *jiaoli* (Collation and reordering of the *Sun Zi* with eleven commentaries). Xinbian zhuzi jicheng (Newly edited collection of the various schools of thought), 1. Beijing: Zhonghua shuju.

Yang Hong. 1992. *Weapons in Ancient China*. New York, Beijing: Science Press, 1992.

———. 2005. *Gudai bingqi tonglun* (General survey of ancient Chinese weaponry). Zhongguo kaogu wenwu tonglun congshu (General surveys of Chinese archaeology and cultural relics of China). Beijing: Zijin Cheng Chuban She.

Yates, Robin D. S. 1980. "The City Under Siege: Technology and Organization as Seen in the Reconstructed Text of the Military Chapters of the Mo-tzu." Ph.D. diss., Harvard University.

———. 1982. "Siege Engines and Late Zhou Military Technology." In *Explorations in the History of Science and Technology*, ed. Hu Daojing (T. C. Hu), Li Guohao, Zhang Mengwen, and Cao Tianqin, 409–52. Compiled in Honour of the Eightieth Birthday of Dr. Joseph Needham. A Special Number of the "Collection of Essays on Chinese Literature and History." Shanghai: Shanghai Chinese Classics.

———. 1988. "New Light on Ancient Chinese Military Texts: Notes on Their Nature and Evolution and the Development of Military Specialization in Warring States China." *T'oung Pao* 74, nos. 4–5:211–48.

Yinque Shan Hanmu Zhujian Zhengli Xiaozu (Yinque Shan Han Tomb Bamboo Strip Manuscripts Study Group), ed. 1975. *Sun Bin bingfa* (Sun Bin's military methods). Beijing: Wenwu Chubanshe.

——, ed. 1976. *Sun Zi bingfa* (Master Sun's military methods). Beijing: Wenwu Chubanshe.

——, ed. 1985. *Yinque Shan Hanmu zhujian* (Bamboo strip manuscripts from the Han tomb at Yinque Shan). Vol. 1. Beijing: Wenwu Chubanshe.

Zhang Dainian. 2002. *Key Concepts in Chinese Philosophy.* Trans. Edmund Ryden. Beijing: Foreign Languages Press; New Haven, Conn.: Yale University Press.

Zheng Liangshu. 1982. "Lun Sun Zi de zuocheng shidai" (On the date of the writing of the *Sun Zi*). In his *Zhujian boshu lunwen ji* (Collected papers on bamboo strip and silk manuscripts), 47–86. Beijing: Zhonghua Shuju.

Zhongguo Renmin Jiefang Jun Junshi Kexue Yuan, Zhanzheng Lilun Yanjiu Bu, *Sun Zi* Zhushi Xiaozu (Group for the Annotation and Explanation of the *Sun Zi* in the Institute for War Theory of the Chinese Peoples Liberation Army Academy of Military Science). 1996 [1977]. *Sun Zi bingfa xinzhu* (Master Sun's military methods, newly annotated). Beijing: Zhonghua Shuju.

Zhou Wei. 2006 [1957]. *Zhongguo bingqi shigao* (A draft history of Chinese weaponry). Rev. and enlgd. ed. Tianjin: Baihua Wenyi Chubanshe.

Zhou Youguang. 1991. "The Family of Chinese Character-Type Scripts (Twenty Members and Four Stages of Development)." *Sino-Platonic Papers* 28 (September): 1–11.

Translations from the Asian Classics

Major Plays of Chikamatsu, tr. Donald Keene 1961

Four Major Plays of Chikamatsu, tr. Donald Keene. Paperback ed. only. 1961; rev. ed. 1997

Records of the Grand Historian of China, translated from the Shih chi of Ssu-ma Ch'ien, tr. Burton Watson, 2 vols. 1961

Instructions for Practical Living and Other Neo-Confucian Writings by Wang Yang-ming, tr. Wing-tsit Chan 1963

Hsün Tzu: Basic Writings, tr. Burton Watson, paperback ed. only. 1963; rev. ed. 1996

Chuang Tzu: Basic Writings, tr. Burton Watson, paperback ed. only. 1964; rev. ed. 1996

The Mahābhārata, tr. Chakravarthi V. Narasimhan. Also in paperback ed. 1965; rev. ed. 1997

The Manyōshū, Nippon Gakujutsu Shinkōkai edition 1965

Su Tung-p'o: Selections from a Sung Dynasty Poet, tr. Burton Watson. Also in paperback ed. 1965

Bhartrihari: Poems, tr. Barbara Stoler Miller. Also in paperback ed. 1967

Basic Writings of Mo Tzu, Hsün Tzu, and Han Fei Tzu, tr. Burton Watson. Also in separate paperback eds. 1967

The Awakening of Faith, Attributed to Aśvaghosha, tr. Yoshito S. Hakeda. Also in paperback ed. 1967

Reflections on Things at Hand: The Neo-Confucian Anthology, comp. Chu Hsi and Lü Tsu-ch'ien, tr. Wing-tsit Chan 1967

The Platform Sutra of the Sixth Patriarch, tr. Philip B. Yampolsky. Also in paperback ed. 1967

Essays in Idleness: The Tsurezuregusa of Kenkō, tr. Donald Keene. Also in paperback ed. 1967

The Pillow Book of Sei Shōnagon, tr. Ivan Morris, 2 vols. 1967

Two Plays of Ancient India: The Little Clay Cart and the Minister's Seal, tr. J. A. B. van Buitenen 1968

The Complete Works of Chuang Tzu, tr. Burton Watson 1968

The Romance of the Western Chamber (Hsi Hsiang chi), tr. S. I. Hsiung. Also in paperback ed. 1968

The Manyōshū, Nippon Gakujutsu Shinkōkai edition. Paperback ed. only. 1969

Records of the Historian: Chapters from the Shih chi of Ssu-ma Ch'ien, tr. Burton Watson. Paperback ed. only. 1969

Cold Mountain: 100 Poems by the T'ang Poet Han-shan, tr. Burton Watson. Also in paperback ed. 1970

Twenty Plays of the Nō Theatre, ed. Donald Keene. Also in paperback ed. 1970

Chūshingura: The Treasury of Loyal Retainers, tr. Donald Keene. Also in paperback ed. 1971; rev. ed. 1997

The Zen Master Hakuin: Selected Writings, tr. Philip B. Yampolsky 1971

Chinese Rhyme-Prose: Poems in the Fu Form from the Han and Six Dynasties Periods, tr. Burton Watson. Also in paperback ed. 1971

Kūkai: Major Works, tr. Yoshito S. Hakeda. Also in paperback ed. 1972

The Old Man Who Does as He Pleases: Selections from the Poetry and Prose of Lu Yu, tr. Burton Watson 1973

The Lion's Roar of Queen Śrīmālā, tr. Alex and Hideko Wayman 1974

Courtier and Commoner in Ancient China: Selections from the History of the Former Han by Pan Ku, tr. Burton Watson. Also in paperback ed. 1974

Japanese Literature in Chinese, vol. 1: Poetry and Prose in Chinese by Japanese Writers of the Early Period, tr. Burton Watson 1975

Japanese Literature in Chinese, vol. 2: Poetry and Prose in Chinese by Japanese Writers of the Later Period, tr. Burton Watson 1976

Scripture of the Lotus Blossom of the Fine Dharma, tr. Leon Hurvitz. Also in paperback ed. 1976

Love Song of the Dark Lord: Jayadeva's Gītagovinda, tr. Barbara Stoler Miller. Also in paperback ed. Cloth ed. includes critical text of the Sanskrit. 1977; rev. ed. 1997

Ryōkan: Zen Monk-Poet of Japan, tr. Burton Watson 1977

Calming the Mind and Discerning the Real: From the Lam rim chen mo of Tsoṇkha-pa, tr. Alex Wayman 1978

The Hermit and the Love-Thief: Sanskrit Poems of Bhartrihari and Bilhan.a, tr. Barbara Stoler Miller 1978

The Lute: Kao Ming's P'i-p'a chi, tr. Jean Mulligan. Also in paperback ed. 1980

A Chronicle of Gods and Sovereigns: Jinnō Shōtōki of Kitabatake Chikafusa, tr. H. Paul Varley 1980

Among the Flowers: The Hua-chien chi, tr. Lois Fusek 1982

Grass Hill: Poems and Prose by the Japanese Monk Gensei, tr. Burton Watson 1983

Doctors, Diviners, and Magicians of Ancient China: Biographies of Fang-shih, tr. Kenneth J. DeWoskin. Also in paperback ed. 1983

Theater of Memory: The Plays of Kālidāsa, ed. Barbara Stoler Miller. Also in paperback ed. 1984

The Columbia Book of Chinese Poetry: From Early Times to the Thirteenth Century, ed. and tr. Burton Watson. Also in paperback ed. 1984

Poems of Love and War: From the Eight Anthologies and the Ten Long Poems of Classical Tamil, tr. A. K. Ramanujan. Also in paperback ed. 1985

The Bhagavad Gita: Krishna's Counsel in Time of War, tr. Barbara Stoler Miller 1986

The Columbia Book of Later Chinese Poetry, ed. and tr. Jonathan Chaves. Also in paperback ed. 1986

The Tso Chuan: Selections from China's Oldest Narrative History, tr. Burton Watson 1989

Waiting for the Wind: Thirty-six Poets of Japan's Late Medieval Age, tr. Steven Carter 1989

Selected Writings of Nichiren, ed. Philip B. Yampolsky 1990

Saigyō, Poems of a Mountain Home, tr. Burton Watson 1990

The Book of Lieh Tzu: A Classic of the Tao, tr. A. C. Graham. Morningside ed. 1990

The Tale of an Anklet: An Epic of South India—The Cilappatikāram of Ilaṇkō Aṭikaḷ, tr. R. Parthasarathy 1993

Waiting for the Dawn: A Plan for the Prince, tr. with introduction by Wm. Theodore de Bary 1993

Yoshitsune and the Thousand Cherry Trees: A Masterpiece of the Eighteenth-Century Japanese Puppet Theater, tr., annotated, and with introduction by Stanleigh H. Jones, Jr. 1993

The Lotus Sutra, tr. Burton Watson. Also in paperback ed. 1993

The Classic of Changes: A New Translation of the I Ching as Interpreted by Wang Bi, tr. Richard John Lynn 1994

Beyond Spring: Tz'u Poems of the Sung Dynasty, tr. Julie Landau 1994

The Columbia Anthology of Traditional Chinese Literature, ed. Victor H. Mair 1994

Scenes for Mandarins: The Elite Theater of the Ming, tr. Cyril Birch 1995

Letters of Nichiren, ed. Philip B. Yampolsky; tr. Burton Watson et al. 1996

Unforgotten Dreams: Poems by the Zen Monk Shōtetsu, tr. Steven D. Carter 1997

The Vimalakirti Sutra, tr. Burton Watson 1997

Japanese and Chinese Poems to Sing: The Wakan rōei shū, tr. J. Thomas Rimer and Jonathan Chaves 1997

Breeze Through Bamboo: Kanshi of Ema Saikō, tr. Hiroaki Sato 1998

A Tower for the Summer Heat, by Li Yu, tr. Patrick Hanan 1998

Traditional Japanese Theater: An Anthology of Plays, by Karen Brazell 1998

The Original Analects: Sayings of Confucius and His Successors (0479–0249), by E. Bruce Brooks and A. Taeko Brooks 1998

The Classic of the Way and Virtue: A New Translation of the Tao-te ching of Laozi as Interpreted by Wang Bi, tr. Richard John Lynn 1999

Modern Chinese Stories and Novellas, 1919–1949, ed. Joseph S. M. Lau, C. T. Hsia, and Leo Ou-fan Lee. Also in paperback ed. 1984

A View by the Sea, by Yasuoka Shōtarō, tr. Kären Wigen Lewis 1984

Other Worlds: Arishima Takeo and the Bounds of Modern Japanese Fiction, by Paul Anderer 1984

Selected Poems of Sō Chōngju, tr. with introduction by David R. McCann 1989

The Sting of Life: Four Contemporary Japanese Novelists, by Van C. Gessel 1989

Stories of Osaka Life, by Oda Sakunosuke, tr. Burton Watson 1990

The Bodhisattva, or Samantabhadra, by Ishikawa Jun, tr. with introduction by William Jefferson Tyler 1990

The Travels of Lao Ts'an, by Liu T'ieh-yün, tr. Harold Shadick. Morningside ed. 1990

Three Plays by Kōbō Abe, tr. with introduction by Donald Keene 1993

The Columbia Anthology of Modern Chinese Literature, ed. Joseph S. M. Lau and Howard Goldblatt 1995

Modern Japanese Tanka, ed. and tr. Makoto Ueda 1996

Masaoka Shiki: Selected Poems, ed. and tr. Burton Watson 1997

Writing Women in Modern China: An Anthology of Women's Literature from the Early Twentieth Century, ed. and tr. Amy D. Dooling and Kristina M. Torgeson 1998

American Stories, by Nagai Kafū, tr. Mitsuko Iriye 2000

The Paper Door and Other Stories, by Shiga Naoya, tr. Lane Dunlop 2001

Grass for My Pillow, by Saiichi Maruya, tr. Dennis Keene 2002

For All My Walking: Free-Verse Haiku of Taneda Santōka, with Excerpts from His Diaries, tr. Burton Watson 2003

The Columbia Anthology of Modern Japanese Literature, vol. 1: *From Restoration to Occupation, 1868–1945,* ed. J. Thomas Rimer and Van C. Gessel 2005

The Columbia Anthology of Modern Japanese Literature, vol. 2: *From 1945 to the Present,* ed. J. Thomas Rimer and Van C. Gessel 2007

STUDIES IN ASIAN CULTURE

The Ōnin War: History of Its Origins and Background, with a Selective Translation of the Chronicle of Ōnin, by H. Paul Varley 1967

Chinese Government in Ming Times: Seven Studies, ed. Charles O. Hucker 1969

The Actors' Analects (Yakusha Rongo), ed. and tr. Charles J. Dunn and Bungō Torigoe 1969

Self and Society in Ming Thought, by Wm. Theodore de Bary and the Conference on Ming Thought. Also in paperback ed. 1970

A History of Islamic Philosophy, by Majid Fakhry, 2d ed. 1983

Phantasies of a Love Thief: The Caurapañcāśikā Attributed to Bilhan.a, by Barbara Stoler Miller 1971

Iqbal: Poet-Philosopher of Pakistan, ed. Hafeez Malik 1971

The Golden Tradition: An Anthology of Urdu Poetry, ed. and tr. Ahmed Ali. Also in paperback ed. 1973

Conquerors and Confucians: Aspects of Political Change in Late Yüan China, by John W. Dardess 1973

The Unfolding of Neo-Confucianism, by Wm. Theodore de Bary and the Conference on Seventeenth-Century Chinese Thought. Also in paperback ed. 1975

To Acquire Wisdom: The Way of Wang Yang-ming, by Julia Ching 1976

Gods, Priests, and Warriors: The Bhrugus of the Mahābhārata, by Robert P. Goldman 1977

Mei Yao-ch'en and the Development of Early Sung Poetry, by Jonathan Chaves 1976

The Legend of Semimaru, Blind Musician of Japan, by Susan Matisoff 1977

Sir Sayyid Ahmad Khan and Muslim Modernization in India and Pakistan, by Hafeez Malik 1980

The Khilafat Movement: Religious Symbolism and Political Mobilization in India, by Gail Minault 1982

The World of K'ung Shang-jen: A Man of Letters in Early Ch'ing China, by Richard Strassberg 1983

The Lotus Boat: The Origins of Chinese Tz'u Poetry in T'ang Popular Culture, by Marsha L. Wagner 1984

Expressions of Self in Chinese Literature, ed. Robert E. Hegel and Richard C. Hessney 1985

Songs for the Bride: Women's Voices and Wedding Rites of Rural India, by W. G. Archer; ed. Barbara Stoler Miller and Mildred Archer 1986

The Confucian Kingship in Korea: Yŏngjo and the Politics of Sagacity, by JaHyun Kim Haboush 1988

Companions to Asian Studies

Approaches to the Oriental Classics, ed. Wm. Theodore de Bary 1959

Early Chinese Literature, by Burton Watson. Also in paperback ed. 1962

Approaches to Asian Civilizations, ed. Wm. Theodore de Bary and Ainslie T. Embree 1964

The Classic Chinese Novel: A Critical Introduction, by C. T. Hsia. Also in paperback ed. 1968

Chinese Lyricism: Shih Poetry from the Second to the Twelfth Century, tr. Burton Watson. Also in paperback ed. 1971

A Syllabus of Indian Civilization, by Leonard A. Gordon and Barbara Stoler Miller 1971

Twentieth-Century Chinese Stories, ed. C. T. Hsia and Joseph S. M. Lau. Also in paperback ed. 1971

A Syllabus of Chinese Civilization, by J. Mason Gentzler, 2d ed. 1972

A Syllabus of Japanese Civilization, by H. Paul Varley, 2d ed. 1972

An Introduction to Chinese Civilization, ed. John Meskill, with the assistance of J. Mason Gentzler 1973

An Introduction to Japanese Civilization, ed. Arthur E. Tiedemann 1974

Ukifune: Love in the Tale of Genji, ed. Andrew Pekarik 1982

The Pleasures of Japanese Literature, by Donald Keene 1988

A Guide to Oriental Classics, ed. Wm. Theodore de Bary and Ainslie T. Embree; 3d edition ed. Amy Vladeck Heinrich, 2 vols. 1989

INTRODUCTION TO ASIAN CIVILIZATIONS

Wm. Theodore de Bary, General Editor
Sources of Japanese Tradition, 1958; paperback ed., 2 vols., 1964. 2d ed., vol. 1, 2001, compiled by Wm. Theodore de Bary, Donald Keene, George Tanabe, and Paul Varley; vol. 2, 2005, compiled by Wm. Theodore de Bary, Carol Gluck, and Arthur E. Tiedemann; vol. 2, abridged, 2 pts., 2006, compiled by Wm. Theodore de Bary, Carol Gluck, and Arthur E. Tiedemann
Sources of Indian Tradition, 1958; paperback ed., 2 vols., 1964. 2d ed., 2 vols., 1988
Sources of Chinese Tradition, 1960, paperback ed., 2 vols., 1964. 2d ed., vol. 1, 1999, compiled by Wm. Theodore de Bary and Irene Bloom; vol. 2, 2000, compiled by Wm. Theodore de Bary and Richard Lufrano
Sources of Korean Tradition, 1997; 2 vols., vol. 1, 1997, compiled by Peter H. Lee and Wm. Theodore de Bary; vol. 2, 2001, compiled by Yŏngho Ch'oe, Peter H. Lee, and Wm. Theodore de Bary

NEO-CONFUCIAN STUDIES

Instructions for Practical Living and Other Neo-Confucian Writings by Wang Yang-ming, tr. Wing-tsit Chan 1963
Reflections on Things at Hand: The Neo-Confucian Anthology, comp. Chu Hsi and Lü Tsu-ch'ien, tr. Wing-tsit Chan 1967
Self and Society in Ming Thought, by Wm. Theodore de Bary and the Conference on Ming Thought. Also in paperback ed. 1970
The Unfolding of Neo-Confucianism, by Wm. Theodore de Bary and the Conference on Seventeenth-Century Chinese Thought. Also in paperback ed. 1975
Principle and Practicality: Essays in Neo-Confucianism and Practical Learning, ed. Wm. Theodore de Bary and Irene Bloom. Also in paperback ed. 1979
The Syncretic Religion of Lin Chao-en, by Judith A. Berling 1980
The Renewal of Buddhism in China: Chu-hung and the Late Ming Synthesis, by Chün-fang Yü 1981
Neo-Confucian Orthodoxy and the Learning of the Mind-and-Heart, by Wm. Theodore de Bary 1981
Yüan Thought: Chinese Thought and Religion Under the Mongols, ed. Hok-lam Chan and Wm. Theodore de Bary 1982
The Liberal Tradition in China, by Wm. Theodore de Bary 1983
The Development and Decline of Chinese Cosmology, by John B. Henderson 1984
The Rise of Neo-Confucianism in Korea, by Wm. Theodore de Bary and JaHyun Kim Haboush 1985
Chiao Hung and the Restructuring of Neo-Confucianism in Late Ming, by Edward T. Ch'ien 1985